Murder & Crime

NOTTINGHAM

Murder & Crime

NOTTINGHAM

ADAM NIGHTINGALE

TEMPUS

To Mama, the first time didn't count. The boy's still a fool.

Frontispiece: Two boys, aged eleven and thirteen years, sentenced to five days' hard labour in 1899 for the crime of causing wilful damage to a door. (Courtesy of the Galleries of Justice, taken from *The Prison Service in Britain* (2006) by Beverley Baker and Laura Butler)

First published 2007

Tempus Publishing
Cirencester Road, Chalford,
Stroud, Gloucestershire, GL6 8PE
www.tempus-publishing.com

Tempus Publishing is an imprint of NPI Media Group

© Adam Nightingale, 2007

The right of Adam Nightingale to be identified as the Author of this work has been asserted in accordance with the Copyrights, Designs and Patents Act 1988.

All rights reserved. No part of this book may be reprinted or reproduced or utilised in any form or by any electronic, mechanical or other means, now known or hereafter invented, including photocopying and recording, or in any information storage or retrieval system, without the permission in writing from the Publishers.

British Library Cataloguing in Publication Data.
A catalogue record for this book is available from the British Library.

ISBN 978 07524 4496 3

Typesetting and origination by NPI Media Group
Printed in Great Britain

Contents

	Acknowledgements	6
1	'Some Unknown and Evil Enemy': Nottingham Castle and the Fall of Roger Mortimer	7
2	The Sins of Nottingham: the Rise and Fall of a Nottingham Exorcist	16
3	Thunder Gun: Nottingham and Highway Robbery	24
4	Malin Hill: the Theft of a Set of Curtains Spirals into Something a Little More Serious…	32
5	The Terror of an Example: the Terminal Aftermath of a Public Execution	35
6	A Disorderly Radical City: a Brief History of Rioting in Nottingham	42
7	Manly Conduct: a Nottingham Prize-Fighter, his Esteemed Mentor and Brutal Rivals	50
8	Life and Death of a County Gaol	58
9	Mr and Mrs Thompson: How a Nottingham Girl Dethroned the King of Cat Burglars	68
10	Pierrepoint and the Low Part of Town: a Concise History of Nottingham's Most Notorious Slum and How it Helped Establish a Baleful Family Enterprise	76
	Bibliography	89
	A Gallery of Punishments and Prison Life	91

Acknowledgements

Credits:
Illustrations by Stephen Dennis.
Portraits of Richard Bancroft, Charles Peace and Henry Pierrepoint by Jean Nightingale.
'Old Nottingham Castle' by Peter Nightingale.
Contemporary photographs by Mark Nightingale (with additional images taken by the author).
Archive images courtesy of Nottingham City Council, www.picturethepast.org.uk and the Nottingham Historical Film Unit.
The author also wishes to acknowledge the assistance of the Galleries of Justice, whose valuable and generous help contributed greatly to the writing of this book.

Thanks to Bev Baker, Katy Archer and Laura Dean for recommending me. Cheers also to Bev for lugging antique firearms across empty buildings and making all the physical and archive resources of the Galleries freely available to me. Thanks to Gary and Trev for letting Mark and I on the roof and giving us crucial advice about adjacent hotel windows, Sarah L. Seaton for her terrific research into the common lodging houses of Narrow Marsh, Nick Tomlinson at Picture the Past, Paul Baker, Susannah Nightingale, Steve and Rachael Roberts, Hazle Wardle, Gio Baffa, Cheryl Gill, Laura Butler and Malcolm Bibby, who have all provided important encouragement, technical and moral support. A final heartfelt thanks to my editors at Tempus, Laura Coulman and Cate Ludlow. Thanks.

I

'Some Unknown and Evil Enemy': Nottingham Castle and the Fall of Roger Mortimer

Compared to its past glories, Nottingham Castle is the diminished article, demolished by the Roundheads in the Civil War and gutted by fire during the Reform Bill Riots of 1831. But the castle was once one of the key fortresses in medieval England and considered by many to be impregnable. Built by William the Conqueror to consolidate his victory over the Saxons, Nottingham Castle was expanded and reinforced over the successive generations to a formidable degree. In the numerous internecine squabbles of the twelfth century, in which siege warfare was a common tactic, Nottingham Castle was never taken. When the Earl of Gloucester burned Nottingham in 1140 he could not breach the castle walls. And when the city was torched thirteen years later, the Duke of Normandy felt that any assault on the castle was a pointless waste of life and materials. Richard the Lionheart failed to take it by force but hanged rebels in front of its walls. His successor and rival, King John, hanged them from the actual battlements. Its history was a bloody one before the advent of the fourteenth century. But the crowning of Edward II in 1307 would make Nottingham Castle the fulcrum around which one of the most insidious and grisly royal feuds in English history would be resolved.

Edward I was a brutal but effective war leader. His reign was defined by wars with the Welsh and the Scots. He understood perfectly the geographic and strategic value of Nottingham Castle. Its vantage point in the centre of his kingdom made it an ideal store for supplies. It also acted as a holding place for prisoners of war. Edward spent a fortune maintaining and strengthening the Midlands fortress.

In 1297 his armies fared badly against the Scottish warlord William Wallace, suffering humiliating defeat at the Battle of Stirling Bridge. Edward sought retribution, commanding the field in person. He defeated Wallace one year later at Falkirk. Wallace escaped capture but was no longer a significant threat. Edward began to take Scotland back piece by piece. It was violent suppression: the combination of mass hangings and the sacking of key castles sapped the strength and appetite for war of Edward's enemies. So much so that, when Edward offered amnesty for any noble that pledged allegiance to him, Scotland capitulated. Wallace was betrayed by his own people. He was captured and taken to London, where he was executed. Edward reserved for Wallace a form of public execution that he had personally introduced to the statue books – that of hanging, drawing and quartering. In 1305 the Scottish rebel was publicly disembowelled before a mob of jubilant Londoners at Smithfields.

As soon as it seemed that the Scottish problem had been resolved, a new and wily enemy emerged to plague the English; Scottish nobleman and claimant to her throne Robert the Bruce

A rooftop view of Nottingham Castle.

rebelled against Edward. Bruce had the sense not to face the king in open battle and conducted a successful hit-and-run campaign of proto-guerrilla warfare. The contest between the two nations was not to be resolved in the king's lifetime. In 1307 the king died leaving his son Edward to rule in his place. It was a strategic gift to the Scots.

Edward II was not fit to reign. His relationship with his father had been traumatic. The former king had not been shy of physically attacking his son, at one point tearing Edward's hair out of his head. Young Edward was good-looking and athletic but regarded as less than a man by his father. His preferred hobbies of thatching, acting and rowing were perceived as effeminate. His father's deepest contempt was reserved for Edward's intense male friendships, particularly his association with the young nobleman Piers Gaveston. It was commonly believed that their relationship was a sexual one, anathema to the morals of the time.

It is hard not to sympathise with the young king born to an abusive father, not temperamentally suited to the vicious rigours of medieval statesmanship and possessed of a sexual orientation that earned him the murderous contempt of his peers – but Edward was an appalling monarch nevertheless. His flagrant favouring of Gaveston in the dispensation of titles, power and influence at court alienated the nobles whose support he needed to administer his kingdom. The internal instability Edward provoked amongst his subjects manifested itself in Nottingham in the form of a dispute that resulted in the murder of the mayor and an assault on the royal castle. In 1312, five years into Edward's reign, the nobles served their own referendum on their new monarch by killing Gaveston.

Perhaps Edward's domestic blunders might have been forgiven by his subjects had he been a successful war leader. But Edward II was about to serve the nation one of their most humiliating military defeats. Robert the Bruce, who had avoided openly clashing with Edward's father, now felt confident enough to tackle his son in a pitched battle despite being outnumbered three to one. Robert the Bruce was everything that Edward was not: a skilled strategist and an inspiring orator with almost miraculous powers of statesmanship. He united the Scottish nobility behind him despite blatantly murdering a prominent and popular rival in the squabble for Scottish succession.

Old Nottingham Castle.

The two armies met at Bannockburn in 1314. Edward showed great personal bravery in close combat but virtually no leadership. Amongst his many blunders, he catastrophically failed to commit his Welsh and Gascon archers – warriors that may have swung the battle in his favour – until it was far too late. The Bruce's army killed 4,000 English soldiers and secured Scotland for the Scottish for centuries to come. It was the only time in history that an English army had fallen to the Scots when the king had commanded them on the field of battle.

Edward had an almost pathological inability to learn from his past mistakes. With Gaveston dead, Edward found another unpopular favourite in the young nobleman Hugh Despenser. As with Gaveston, Edward preferred Despenser's interests over others' at court. In one instance, an area of land in Wales became the bone of contention. The Despenser family claimed Gower as their own, though other nobles disputed the claim. Prominent among them was Roger Mortimer.

Mortimer had been a reasonably loyal subject up to that point. Edward had awarded him the title Lieutenant of Ireland and he had fought Robert the Bruce's brother (another Edward) in an abortive attempt to drive the English out of Ireland. Mortimer had been bequeathed lands in Wales and felt, along with many others, that the Despenser family's claims were in conflict with his own. So, when the king clearly favoured Despenser to the exclusion of all others, he made a powerful enemy and helped forge the circumstances of his own destruction.

By the 1320s, the dispute between the Despensers and the Mortimer-backed coalition known as the Marcher Lords had degenerated into open warfare. Although the Marcher Lords were keen to point out that their argument was not with the king himself but merely an attempt to protect him from an insidious influence threatening to the country as a whole, the king nevertheless regarded them as traitors. An attack on Despenser was an attack on the king. The rebellion failed and Mortimer and his uncle were forced to give themselves up. Both men were convicted of treason, sentenced to death, and locked away in the Tower of London.

By this point Edward had not only alienated his allies but his wife. Edward had married Isabella, the daughter of Phillip IV of France in 1308. Understandably it was not a particularly happy marriage. Gaveston's presence in the early stages of their relationship must have been a constant source of humiliation to the young bride. Whether the relationship between Edward and his favourite was a sexual one or not, Isabella only began to conceive children with the king after Gaveston's murder. The advent of Despenser exacerbated tensions between the couple. Isabella felt that her own interests and wishes were being usurped in favour of the king's new favourite. By the 1320s, in the light of the current civil conflict, Edward sent his wife to the Tower for her own safety.

The Spartan conditions of the Tower took their toll on Mortimer's uncle, who died before he could be executed. Mortimer's own sentence was commuted to life imprisonment. Mortimer and the queen were present in the Tower at the same time; many suspected a romantic liaison between the two. Some saw Isabella's influence in the decision not to execute Mortimer. What happened next sparked further rumours of collusion between the queen and the rebellious nobleman – Mortimer escaped.

The more fanciful accounts of his flight have Mortimer climbing up the kitchen chimney, descending the tower walls on a rope ladder and crossing the Thames in a rowing boat, his escape aided and abetted by a love-struck queen who had doped the guards with a powerful sleeping draft. How he actually got out remains a mystery, but his escape is historic fact. Roger Mortimer fled the Tower and, together with his loyal compatriot Richard Monmouth, left the country and took refuge in Paris.

Edward II did not need anything else to complicate a reign already overburdened with incompetent blundering, but in 1324 he had found himself on the verge of a badly timed and deeply unwanted war with France. A Gascon vassal of Edward's had somehow taken it upon himself to sack the French fortress of Saint Sardos. Skilful diplomacy was called for to avert open war. Edward decided to send his wife to parley with her brother Charles IV. Isabella agreed and left with her son Edward, the heir to the throne. Isabella and Mortimer were reunited in Paris. If there was any ambiguity about the nature of their relationship in England, all doubts were banished when they openly declared themselves lovers in the court of the French king. The union spelled destruction for the king of England, the irony being that he had facilitated it all himself.

A passionate correspondence between the king and his estranged wife saw Edward pleading for reconciliation and the return of his son. He also condemned Mortimer, referring to him as 'our traitor and mortal foe' and 'some unknown and evil enemy'. In her replies, Isabella denounced the Despensers but Edward continued to defend them. Mortimer and Isabella planned to come back to England, but this time they would have an army with them and proposed to take the throne by force.

Edward prepared for war. He tried to refortify his defences but couldn't secure the funds. He brought the weight of the Church to bear on the French court, enlisting the help of bishops and ultimately the Pope in an attempt to persuade Charles to withdraw finance and troops for the ensuing war. Ultimately it was a generous bribe from the Despensers that choked off any financial, military and moral support from the French monarch, who subsequently banished his sister and threatened any nobleman who aided her or Mortimer. But one thing that typified Edward's reign was an overabundance of volunteers to frustrate the interests of the king of England. Isabella and Mortimer found martial patronage from the Count of Hainault.

In 1326 the invasion was launched. When it happened, it was distinguished by an abject lack of resistance from Edward's subjects. Edward's navy refused to support him. He posted a £1,000 bounty on Mortimer's head. His wife responded by placing a counter-bounty of £2,000 on Hugh Despenser's head. In a desperate attempt to get anyone to fight for him, Edward offered to pardon any criminal or former traitor who would take arms against the invaders. A wave of anti-Edward rioting, looting and murder erupted in the capital. Edward fled London, his reign effectively at an end.

Hugh Despenser was caught and hung, drawn and quartered. Edward was captured at Kenilworth. He was imprisoned at Berkeley Castle in Gloucester and murdered in secret. Nobody really knows how the king died but contemporary chroniclers spoke of a horrific ordeal in which a heated spike – possibly a poker, a cooking spit, or a cow horn – was inserted into his anus. If true, the choice of murder weapon was either a sadistic black joke at the expense of his alleged homosexuality, or else a pragmatic but vile method of leaving no external signs of trauma. It was also rumoured that the king had been refused the sacrament before his death, arguably confining him to hell post-despatch. His death was reported officially as a 'fatal accident'. His son was crowned Edward III in January 1327. The new king was only fourteen years old.

For the next three years Isabella and Mortimer reigned as *de facto* king and queen of England. However, anybody hoping for a utopian reign of peace and unification augmented by victories against foreign enemies was to be bitterly disappointed: Mortimer and Isabella proved as corrupt and diplomatically incompetent as the monarch and his cohorts that they had gone to such great lengths to remove. Despenser's lands were seized and Mortimer claimed for himself the titles of Justice of Wales and Earl of March. The young king's uncle was executed for treason on very spurious grounds. Mortimer and Isabella launched an invasion of Scotland so catastrophic that they were obliged to sign a treaty recognising their old enemy Robert the Bruce's right to kingship, as well as a complete renunciation of any English claim to the Scottish crown and lands. For their efforts, Mortimer and Isabella received a £20,000 gratuity from the Bruce. Technically the money belonged to England, but much of it found its way into Mortimer and Isabella's own pockets.

A regency council was established. Mortimer took no official place on this council but his wishes were executed through sympathetic or puppet council members and his was the dominant voice in government. He was also considered untouchable by would-be assassins, as he never went anywhere without a retinue of Welsh mercenaries.

In 1330, the council met in Nottingham and the final chapter of the ugly vendetta was to be played out in the shadow of the old Norman castle.

Young Edward was approaching his eighteenth birthday. His mother had become pregnant by Mortimer. Edward held Mortimer personally responsible for the murder of his father and, in the light of his mother's pregnancy, feared that he himself might soon be assassinated. A barely suppressed atmosphere of mutual recrimination was rife between the king and his guardian. Edward was understandably nervous about his own future. Fortunately, he had a powerful ally in the fiery nobleman Montague. Edward had the inclination to act and Montague the strategic know-how. Between them, they began to concoct a plan to remove Mortimer for good.

The Nottingham council brought matters very quickly to a head. Hearing rumours that Edward and nobles sympathetic to his cause were planning to overthrow him, Mortimer turned on the Earl of Lancaster, a noble known to be sympathetic to the young king. He ordered Lancaster to vacate Nottingham and take up a position of safety two to three miles outside of the town. Lancaster was hardly a personal threat to Mortimer as he was reasonably old and virtually blind and it was an action correctly perceived as that of a cornered man lashing out at the easiest available target. Much more dangerous was Montague. Whether it was in Mortimer's presence or in public is not clear, but Montague was believed to have said aloud what most people at the time were thinking: that Mortimer had murdered King Edward II. For Mortimer this was intolerable. On 19 October, Montague was summoned before a tribunal and accused of treason. It prompted a heated exchange in which Montague asserted his loyalty to the true king. Mortimer stated that at present his word outranked that of the king when there was a conflict of opinion. Mortimer, Montague and, by implication, Edward had laid their cards on the table. The three men were beyond any form of arbitration; their situation mutually untenable. In private, Montague spurred his king to immediate and violent action stating that, 'it was better that they should eat the dog than let the dog eat them.'

Mortimer was fearful of attack and moved Isabella and Edward into Nottingham Castle. At this stage he must have felt reasonably secure; he had separated Edward from Montague and he was surrounded by his personal bodyguards in a castle with an impeccable reputation for having never been breached. In addition to this, at Mortimer's beck and call were two capable warriors loyal unto death: Hugh de Turpington and Richard Monmouth, the man who had partnered Mortimer in his spectacular escape from the Tower of London. All the gates were barred, the doors locked and Isabella kept the keys on her person. No one could possibly enter.

Montague's secret weapon was local constable William d'Eland, an official loyal to the king, resident within the castle and in possession of damaging knowledge; William knew of a secret entrance to the castle kitchen that circumvented Mortimer's private army and would place a small band of soldiers in the heart of the fortress. He had agreed to ensure that a postern gate at the base of the cliff beneath the castle ramparts would be left open, giving the attackers access to the tunnel. In case there was any doubt as to William's loyalty, Edward threatened him with violence should he fail to uphold his part of the bargain.

On the evening of the 19th, Montague left Nottingham in a hurry, feigning flight for fear of his life. He reassembled close to midnight in the park beneath the castle with close to two-dozen armed men. Montague's intention was to rendezvous with a second force. The reinforcements did not materialise. They later claimed to have been lost in the forest surrounding the castle but many believe that panic got the better of them. Nevertheless, Montague pressed on with the men he had. William d'Eland was as good as his word: the postern gate was open and the small band of armed men entered the narrow passageway and began to climb the steps.

Mortimer and many of those loyal to him were in a hall near to Isabella's bedchamber. Edward feigned illness (possibly with the complicity of his physician). He excused himself from his mother's presence, pretending to go to bed. Instead, he made his way to the kitchen and waited there for Montague. When Montague arrived, Edward directed the band up the thin staircase that led to the hall where Mortimer reclined.

Perhaps the sound of clanking weaponry was audible in the hall, for Montague's men were heard coming up the staircase. It was too late to call on the Welsh for immediate help; Mortimer's salvation rested in the fighting prowess of his two chosen men and whether they could hold off the forces on the narrow stairs until the mercenaries arrived. Turpington and Monmouth bravely clashed with the invaders and a brief but bloody skirmish ensued. Turpington's skull was smashed to pieces with a mace. Monmouth was stabbed to death.

There was very little Mortimer could do as the royal hall filled up with armed men. Isabella screamed for mercy on behalf of her lover as he was dragged out of the castle.

What had been done in secret was celebrated in public the following day as the reviled Mortimer was led through the streets of Nottingham on his way back to London and the Tower. There would be no repeat of history: this time Mortimer would not escape. Edward had been all for killing Mortimer on the spot but Lancaster had advised the king not to commit murder but to deal with Mortimer through the channels permitted by law. The king acquiesced. The penalties permitted by law were grim enough: Mortimer could be hung, drawn and quartered. A summary execution might have been kinder, but Edward was determined not to duplicate the errors of his father or his guardian. He would not kill anyone in private and pretend that they had met with a 'fatal accident'. He would curb the retributive impulses that seemed to typify the ascendance of a new king. Edward confiscated his mother's lands but permitted her a generous allowance. He made a point of only executing one of Mortimer's supporters. Roger Mortimer's fate, however, was sealed. His trial was a formality, with Mortimer presented to the court bound and gagged and forbidden to speak in his own defence. He was convicted of regicide and sentenced to death.

Above: Nottingham Castle viewed from the dark woods where Montague hid, waiting to infiltrate the medieval fortress.

Below: Openings in the sandstone rock at the base of Nottingham Castle, similar to those that gave entrance to Montague and his small force of soldiers.

Montague leads his band of soldiers into the castle via a secret passageway.

Whether out of deference for his mother's feelings, or a keenness to present himself as a monarch who understood the currency of relative clemency, Edward spared Mortimer the agony of disembowelment.

Mortimer was led through the streets of London forcibly dressed in the clothes he had worn at the funeral of Edward II. He was stripped naked and hanged. His body was left suspended for two days before it was cut down. Roger Mortimer set a dubious legal precedent in being the first English nobleman hanged in public at Tyburn Gallows – a commoner's death.

On his way to the gallows, these verses from the Bible were quoted over him:

1: Why boastest thou thyself in mischief, O mighty man? the goodness of God endureth continually.
2: Thy tongue deviseth mischiefs; like a sharp rasor, working deceitfully.
3: Thou lovest evil more than good; and lying rather than to speak righteousness. Selah.
4: Thou lovest all devouring words, O thou deceitful tongue.
5: God shall likewise destroy thee for ever, he shall take thee away, and pluck thee out of thy dwelling place, and root thee out of the land of the living. Selah.
6: The righteous also shall see, and fear, and shall laugh at him.
7: Lo, this is the man that made not God his strength; but trusted in the abundance of his riches, and strengthened himself in his wickedness.
8: But I am like a green olive tree in the house of God: I trust in the mercy of God for ever and ever.
9: I will praise thee for ever, because thou hast done it: and I will wait on thy name; for it is good before thy saints.

It was the great psalm of divine vengeance written by David the Old Testament monarch, against his enemy Doeg, mass murderer and failed assassin of the true anointed king.

Montague confronts Roger Mortimer inside the royal halls of Nottingham Castle.

2

The Sins of Nottingham: the Rise and Fall of a Nottingham Exorcist

During the last few years of the reign of Queen Elizabeth I, England was in the throes of a hard-fought ideological civil war. Although science and reason were on the ascendancy throughout much of the academic community, a belief in the occult still had a powerful hold on the imaginations of the ignorant and the intelligent alike. Catholicism was illegal and priests of Rome practiced their vocation at the risk of losing their lives. Anglicanism was the orthodox religion. Puritanism was legal but suspect and Puritans were regarded by many as inflammatory heretics, little better than Catholics. Though Puritans could not be openly persecuted, they were often hounded under various legal pretexts. In Scotland Puritanism reigned supreme. King James wrote treatises on witchcraft and burned its Scottish practitioners at the stake. In England Anglicans and Puritans contested for spiritual ascendancy in the pulpits and ecclesiastical courts of the nation. Many theological controversies became touch-fires for religious antagonism, often with tragic consequences. One of the most contentious issues was that of demonic possession and the exorcism of demons. Toward the closing years of the sixteenth century, a Midlands-born Puritan exorcist was to achieve national notoriety. His public contests with the Devil on the streets of Nottingham were to land him in a London gaol, resulting in a change of Church law.

John Darrell was born in Mansfield in 1562. He studied law at Cambridge but failed to complete his education. It is not known why: perhaps the death of his father prompted a return home where Darrell became a farmer. In 1586 he was summoned to help Thomas Beckingham, the Rector of Bilsthorpe, with a case of demonic possession. The victim was a local woman named Catherine Wright.

Both Puritans and Anglicans believed in the existence of demonic spirits that could gain access to a human being and influence their behaviour in fits and blasphemous outbursts. However, Puritans and Anglicans disagreed sharply on how to go about expelling the devils once they had gained possession of a person's soul. Puritans based their theology of exorcism almost exclusively on a biblical text from Mark's Gospel (chapter 9, verse 29), in which Jesus advises his disciples that some particularly powerful demons may be expelled, 'but by prayer and fasting.' So when a case of possession was discovered, the Puritan approach was for everyone, from the victim to those in immediate proximity, to be subjected to a strict regimen of religious devotion and self-denial until the demon had been dislodged. Another factor that typified the Puritan exorcist was the fact that he did not have to be an ordained minister to practice his vocation. With the Anglican Church, the practice of exorcism was strictly reserved for ordained authorities. Although Anglicans, as a rule, were less hasty to read the demonic into a given

Right: John Darrell, Nottingham's controversial Puritan exorcist.

Below: A lady undergoing exorcism singles out a suspected witch.

situation (and vexed by the Puritan impulse to see the Devil in everything), what really offended them were unlicensed, unsolicited, do-it-yourself exorcists gadding about the country subverting orthodox Church authority.

Little is known of what actually took place during the exorcism of Catherine Wright, or the methods used by John Darrell. The exorcism was considered successful and should have been a triumph for the young Puritan, but the aftermath was to leave a nasty taste in Darrell's mouth. During the exorcism, Catherine Wright had implicated a woman named Margaret Roper, claiming that Roper was responsible for releasing an army of demons into her. This was effectively an accusation of witchcraft. Bewitchment was perceived as the most common cause of possession and Margaret Roper was arrested on little more than one woman's unsubstantiated say-so. The accusations could have had lethal consequences for Roper, as witchcraft was punishable by death. However, Roper was saved by Godfrey Foljambe, an unusually enlightened magistrate for his time, who turned on Darrell and threatened him with imprisonment for his part in the affair. Darrell escaped gaol but did not practice his vocation again during the magistrate's lifetime. But ten years later, after Foljambe's death, John Darrell once more took up arms against the Devil. This time, the victim was a teenage boy by the name of Thomas Darling.[1]

Thomas Darling, a native of Burton-on-Trent, was thirteen years old and the ward of his grandparents, both strict Puritans. In 1596, Thomas began suffering from fits. As the year progressed the fits became wilder and Darling was given to bouts of screaming and blasphemous pronouncements. Often, he rolled his eyes and fell prone as if dead. After a while, the fits began to draw an audience. During one of his 'episodes', Darling spoke of an unnamed female, accusing her of bewitching him in the nearby woods. Darling's description matched that of a local woman named Alice Goodrich, whose mother Elizabeth Wright had long been suspected of witchcraft. Goodrich was seized and brought before Thomas Darling. When Goodrich denied the charge of witchcraft, Darling began to spasm in her presence. Goodrich was forced to recite the Lord's Prayer but she could not remember the words. It was then disclosed that she had barely taken communion over the course of the past year. Alice's mother was brought in and subjected to a test that would determine whether or not she was a witch. Her hand was to be scratched: if she bled she was guilty, if she failed to bleed she was innocent. The scratch drew blood and both women found themselves subject to a formal trial for witchcraft. Unlike Catherine Wright, Alice Goodrich did not have a progressive magistrate to protect her and she was imprisoned along with her mother. Alice Goodrich died in gaol.

In the eyes of the community, Alice Goodrich's harsh treatment was seemingly justified as Thomas Darling's health resumed to something approximating normality shortly after her incarceration. But before long, Darling suffered a relapse, and more drastic measures were called for – somebody remembered a story about a local man who had driven out a demon some ten years previously.

John Darrell's involvement with Thomas Darling was brief. He arrived and observed the boy. His diagnosis concurred with the opinion of the general public: the boy was demon-possessed. He prescribed a cure in the form of an old-fashioned regimen of prayer and fasting. John Darrell left the boy and within twenty-four hours, his symptoms had vanished, never to resurface.

Although John Darrell was with Thomas Darling for less than a day, the case effectively launched his reputation as an exorcist. The following year, Darrell would be summoned to Lancashire to deal with seven separate cases of possession, all present under a single roof. In this

---

1. In the interim between the Catherine Wright case and the Thomas Darling affair, John Darrell had become an ordained minister, acquiring a further air of legitimacy amongst his Puritan brethren.

instance, as in the Darling case, John Darrell was the last resort, brought in when every other option had been exhausted and numerous lives and reputations had been ruined.

The children of wealthy landowner Nicholas Starkey had begun to exhibit signs of demonic possession. His son John had been subject to uncontrollable bouts of shouting while at school. The boy's sister Anne had begun having fits. Both children convalesced at home as their father spent £200 on doctors' bills. The doctors diagnosed demonic possession but could do nothing to help the children. Nicholas Starkey was desperate and sought the aid of a Roman Catholic priest, an action that could have cost him his life. The priest was unable or unwilling to help him. Next, Starkey approached a local magician named Edmund Hartley. Unlike Alice Goodrich or Margaret Roper, Edmund Hartley was seemingly the real thing, a self-confessed practitioner of the occult. He was also a hectoring, vain and suicidally conceited man who nevertheless held a powerful hold over those around him. It is an indication of Nicholas Starkey's desperation that he not only consented to do business with Hartley but invited him into his home, paid him a retainer and gave him *carte blanche* to do whatever was necessary to liberate his children.

Hartley was prone to violent temper tantrums and outrageous demands for increased payment for his services, eventually demanding his own house and grounds. Rather than curing the children, Hartley's presence seemed to coincide with a possession epidemic. Within a few months, three more young girls resident on the estate, as well as a maid and a spinster friend of the family joined the ranks of the possessed. The house had become a cacophonous hostel for any devil or demon that happened to be in the locality. To complicate matters, Hartley may have been conducting an affair with one of the possessed (the maid) and possibly rebuffed the advances of Margaret Byron (the spinster). Wherever the truth lay, Margaret Byron made accusations of devilry against Hartley. It is unlikely that this was true. Far more damaging was the fact that Hartley had actually tried to engage Nicholas Starkey in a necromantic rite on a journey together through a nearby wood. This would have been neither here nor there had not Starkey clashed with the spurned Margaret Byron's minister. The antipathy between the two men resulted in a determination on the part of the clergyman to try Hartley for witchcraft. Hartley was dragged into court, where it was established that he was unable to recite the Lord's Prayer. Nicholas Starkey gave testimony and his statement recounting a trip to the woods with the magician was enough to ensure the death sentence. The black farce of Edmund Hartley's life climaxed with a botched execution when the rope snapped on the gallows. There was a second attempt, and Hartley was hanged.

Richard Starkey's next port of call was the celebrated occultist and former astronomer to Queen Elizabeth, Dr John Dee. Dee suggested that, after a litany of Roman heretics, quack doctors and deranged avaricious sorcerers, perhaps a Christian minister might be in order this time. John Darrell was called for.

As with the Thomas Darling case, Darrell's time amongst the afflicted was surprisingly brief. He recommended the usual regime of prayer and fasting but at least consented to stay and oversee the exorcism in person this time. Throughout the night John Darrell, with the support of the Starkey household, conducted a lengthy prayer vigil over the seven possessed. When the sun rose the next day, six of the seven had been cured. The one incurable demoniac (a young girl named Jane Ashton) took refuge with a Catholic relative. John Darrell's adventure was written-up and circulated by friend and fellow minister George More, a man who was to bask in Darrell's reflected glory and share his future hardship and humiliation.

Within a year of the Lancashire affair, John Darrell had been appointed assistant curate of St Mary's, Nottingham. It was an influential position in Nottingham's most imposing church. Darrell's presence behind a pulpit would guarantee a crowd and he would exhort large congregations, warning them of the numerous strategies of the Devil and advising them as to the best methods by which to defeat him. Darrell was at the peak of his power and influence when he began to receive letters begging him to intervene in a local case of suspected possession. The

Above: St Mary's church.

Below: The interior of St Mary's, where John Darrell preached his dramatic sermons on demonic possession and exorcism.

victim this time was a young serving boy and musician's apprentice named William Somers. The fits that Somers was subject to eclipsed anything Darrell had previously encountered. There was the usual repertoire of spasms, tics and verbal outbursts: in addition to this, Somers could play dead, go into a trance at a moment's notice and confer with invisible creatures. But what set Somers apart was his apparent ability to send an egg-shaped lump of muscle travelling up and down his body as well as the strange animalistic noises he could emit from deep within his person.

John Darrell held off seeing the boy initially. It was only when Peter Clark, the Mayor of Nottingham, implored Darrell to become involved that the exorcist finally arranged to see Somers in person. The two met and Darrell diagnosed Somers' symptoms as demonic in origin. On 5 November 1597, John Darrell officially declared that he was treating the boy.

This time John Darrell's methods were far more grandiose than on previous occasions. With the full support of Robert Aldridge, the vicar of St Mary's (who technically outranked him), Darrell declared that Somers' possession was a consequence of the sins of Nottingham. He insisted that a day be put aside for fasting and prayer. He gathered about himself a retinue of 150 excitable followers who were given to loudly shouting, 'Lord have mercy on us' at the drop of a hat. This grand show of divine force seemed to have the desired effect, as Somers' fits stopped. Darrell was triumphant.

There was a brief cessation of hostilities between the representatives of God and the Devil. But peace suited neither of them. Somers was a lazy young man addicted to attention. During his exorcism he had been confined to bed and had a constant audience. Normality meant the drudgery of work and the absence of publicity. John Darrell was arguably a vain man who had become addicted to the glory of his office. Darrell forecast that the demon in Somers was merely dormant and would become active sometime soon. Within a short space of time, William Somers resumed his manifestations and the battle was on again.

The successive clashes between Darrell and Somers were conducted before voyeuristic crowds, often containing the cream of Nottingham's political elite. They were loud and grotesque displays, during which Darrell would recount his past glories in the presence of Somers, who would obligingly replicate them in his manifestations for a salivating audience. But there were strange anomalies in Somers' behaviour. For the most part, he genuinely did not seem in control of himself when in the throes of a fit. But his manifestations would often stop when he needed to go to the toilet and would resume once he had answered the call of nature.

Naturally Darrell had his critics – any prominent Puritan was never too far away from any number of livid Anglicans praying for his downfall. But for as long as the town was transfixed by the spectacle of Darrell v. Somers, his enemies could do nothing. So, for a brief moment John Darrell was the most powerful man in Nottingham. But William Somers began to do something that would permanently undermine the exorcist's base of power: he began to name witches, throwing fits in the presence of certain women which would stop the moment that they had passed him by. This was interpreted as the demon within Somers reacting to a kindred evil in the passing female. The unlucky women were perceived to be witches. As a consequence of this sort of behaviour, thirteen were arrested. This was par for the course in an exorcism so long as the victims were poor or eccentric, but Somers did not discriminate. He singled out Alice Freeman, the daughter of a prominent Nottingham Alderman. And in failing to adequately control the Devil in young Somers and allowing Freeman to be publicly humiliated, Darrell had alienated some of his most powerful supporters. Suddenly stripped of the implicit protection of his political allies, Darrell's enemies started to come out of the woodwork. Many of his friends began to desert him. Even his benefactor Robert Aldridge complained about the monotonous predictability of Darrell's one-note demon-obsessed sermons. Aldridge was also critical of the way in which Darrell perpetually made the sins of Nottingham the scapegoat for the Devil's constant reappearance in William Somers.

Somers was clearly becoming a liability. Darrell resorted to secular methods and had Somers taken to the workhouse. Outside of John Darrell's direct control, William Somers said something inflammatory – he confessed that he had been coached on how to stage demonic fits by Darrell himself. Somers' admission was a gift to Nottingham's anti-Darrell contingent. An inquiry was launched to determine whether or not John Darrell was a fraud.

In fact there were two inquiries into the Somers case directed by bishops antagonistic and sympathetic to the Darrell cause. The Puritan Archbishop of York, Mathew Hutton, declared the possession authentic, even going so far as to have pins stuck in the prone form of Somers who, remarkably, showed no signs of pain. Somers seemed to have forgotten his denunciation of Darrell when in the presence of the archbishop. He showed the assembly what they wanted to see and told them what they wanted hear. It would be a characteristic that would define the young man whenever he was in the presence of authority of any description. Darrell was vindicated in part but still had to suffer the indignity of having his preacher's licence rescinded.

The second commission was far more serious. In 1598 John Darrell, along with his right-hand man George More, was called to Lambeth Palace in London, the Anglican capital and the heart of anti-Puritanism. Although no record of the official charges survives, it is fair to surmise that Darrell and More were charged with fraudulently staging an exorcism. In the meantime, both men were stripped of ministerial rights and imprisoned pending the court's verdict and sentencing. Darrell was placed in the Gate House, Westminster, whilst More was locked away in Southwark's notorious Clink Prison. Directing the commission was Richard Bancroft, the Bishop of London, and his hatchet man Samuel Harsnet – both vociferous enemies of all things Puritan.

John Darrell did not stand the remotest chance of getting a fair hearing; ecclesiastical courts were not designed that way. Court rules determined that the accused could neither face their accusers nor submit statements in their own defence. Witnesses would never have been questioned verbally. Instead they would submit a written statement. Any cross-examination would have to be via another written statement. Statements containing unsubstantiated gossip, innuendo or hearsay were completely admissible as evidence. Inconvenient evidence could simply be ignored. Darrell had no legal representation or recourse to defend himself. He would not even have heard the charges being brought against him. Thus John Darrell was utterly at the mercy of a court that was not even remotely objective and also bore him deep ill will. What made matters worse was the fact that any attempt to object to the unfairness of the proceedings would be automatically interpreted as the actions of a rebellious and independent man, thus proving the prosecution's case for them. If found guilty, Darrell and More faced the possibility of being permanently stripped of their ministry and confined to gaol for the rest of their lives.

The court would make its ruling on the strength of the written depositions. But the court was in complete control of which depositions were and were not admissible. Witnesses were called who favoured the case against Darrell. Witnesses who might have provided a more balanced and perhaps sympathetic portrait of Darrell were completely ignored. Nobody from Lancashire was summoned to submit a statement, whilst William Somers' word was taken as gospel. Previously sympathetic Puritans were not so sympathetic when confronted with the full weight of Anglican authority and many of Darrell's friends were now openly critical of him. Thomas Darling was brought to London and intimidated into giving a hostile testimony. He was starved, beaten and forced to watch a public execution with the intimation that his fate would be the same as that of the hanged man if he refused to sign a confession against Darrell.

It is commonly believed that John Darrell and George More were never actually declared guilty, so it is unlikely that any sentence was ever officially passed against them. But the Church had absolute authority over its subjects. They were within their rights to detain each man

John Darrell's nemesis, the aggressively anti-Puritan Bishop of London Richard Bancroft.

indefinitely while they vacillated over which verdict or punishment was appropriate; if those in their custody died whilst waiting for the court to make up their mind, then they died. In 1601, Darrell was finally released from prison. It is not known what happened to More, but there is a strong possibility that he was left to rot in prison where he eventually met his end.

Controversy raged during Darrell's incarceration. Darrell wrote books defending his name, which were widely circulated throughout London; there were counter-publications and a brief war of words erupted over Darrell between Anglicans and Puritans. But interest was short lived. The Anglicans had effectively won. Whether they charged him or not was a moot point now: they had succeeded in undermining his credibility and permanently destroying his reputation.

Darrell returned in disgrace to Mansfield and to his original profession – farming. His later years were virtually silent, although he briefly incurred the wrath of the parish when he was caught preaching without a licence. However, the greatest indignity heaped on him was that of obscurity: John Darrell was forgotten for the most part. When remembered at all, it was mainly as a figure of fun, mercilessly satirised, suffering the scorn of authors such as the playwright Ben Jonson, who wrote these lines about him, taken from *The Devil is an Ass* (1616):

Did you ne'er read, Sir, of Little Darrell's tricks
With the Boy o' Burton and the Seven in Lancashire, Sommers at Nottingham? All these do teach it. And we'll give it out, Sir, that your Wife has bewitch'd you.

But Darrell's true legacy was a piece of Canon Law, written in response to the scandal he helped generate. Canon LXXVII of 1603 states that, in order to conduct an exorcism, a license must be obtained by the bishop of the diocese. It is a law that is still in practice today.

3

Thunder Gun: Nottingham and Highway Robbery

In 1701, two miles outside of Nottingham, a twenty-nine-year-old highwayman stopped a coach on the Derby road. A loud blast sounded from the direction of the coach and the highwayman's horse was shot from beneath him. The occupants of the coach disembarked, many of them producing weapons. About his person the highwayman had eight single-shot pistols within easy reach. Both sides opened fire. Of the five gentlemen and two footmen present, the highwayman managed to kill a gentleman and a footman in the gun battle that followed. For their own part, the victims peppered the highwayman with gunfire. The highwayman was struck a number of times. Weak and wet from loss of blood, he lost his strength and collapsed. He was overpowered, restrained and handed over to the authorities. His name was Timothy Buckley and altogether he had sustained eleven separate bullet wounds.

It is most unlikely that Buckley's opponents were as laden with armaments as the highwayman. Their secret weapon was the blunderbuss (a name derived from the German for 'thunder gun'), a short-barrelled, wide-muzzled rifle that fired up to nine lead balls in a single go. The bullets were designed to spread out and would most likely have hit anything put in front of them if the distance were short enough. It was a weapon that was becoming standard issue amongst coachmen and the best defence against increasingly aggressive highway robbers. It had been the blunderbuss that killed Buckley's horse. Some of the surplus shot that had not embedded itself in horseflesh had probably lodged itself in Buckley's body. The rest of the wounds would have been sustained either from pistol fire or a second shot from the blunderbuss, if time and opportunity had permitted its reloading.

Buckley was tried at Nottingham's Shire Hall. It transpired that he had an elaborate history of robbery and violence behind him. Originally from Stamford in Lincolnshire, Buckley had run away from home and headed for London. He had fallen in with the proverbial bad crowd and embraced the criminal path. According to the Newgate Calendar, Buckley robbed a publican in his home and a doctor in Hyde Park. Buckley's career was interrupted by arrest and, by way of penalty, a spell in the army. He served on the Continent in Flanders (probably where he had learned to shoot so effectively). But army life disagreed with him and Buckley added desertion to his list of offences. He returned to London and avenged himself on the constable responsible for his arrest by raping his wife at gunpoint.

Timothy Buckley graduated to highway robbery. He operated in and around the capital until a botched vendetta against another man who had the temerity to have him arrested made

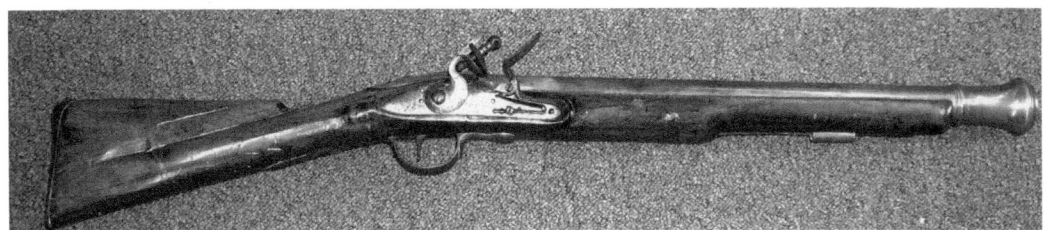

Above: The highly destructive blunderbuss, one of the most effective seventeenth-century deterrents against highway robbery. (Blunderbuss courtesy of the Galleries of Justice)

Right: Highwayman Timothy Buckley gunned down on Derby Road.

London too dangerous a place for Buckley to loiter. He headed for the East Midlands where he managed to rob a house and buy a decent horse before horse and rider were gunned down on the Derby road.

Timothy Buckley was sentenced to death and hanged. His body was placed in a gibbet and displayed on the roadside as a warning to all potential thieves and highway robbers. But despite a litany of colourful and degrading offences, as well as a bloody and spectacular last stand, Buckley's career was considered inauspicious by the criminal standards of the time.

The highwayman was by far the most fashionable of all seventeenth and eighteenth-century criminals. Although highway robbery as a crime predated the likes of Dick Turpin, the highwayman as an entity was very much a product of the reign of Charles I and the Civil War that defined his era. Traditionally highwaymen were believed to have been predominantly upper class and staunchly royalist. The popular and romantic notion of the highwayman was that of an unreconstructed patriot dishing out retribution to the Roundhead overlords who had won the war and killed the king. The highwayman was believed to be chivalrous in conduct and flamboyant in appearance. He was known to rob from the rich and occasionally give to the poor.

Timothy Buckley's dead body was hung in a gibbet similar to this one and displayed publicly on a Nottinghamshire roadside. (Gibbet courtesy of the Galleries of Justice)

In truth, many highwaymen were royalist in sympathy but their motives for taking to the road were wide and varied. The Civil War had taught them how to fight and had inured many of them to brutality. Many had had their lands seized and sought restitution by illegal means. Some had simply become addicted to a lifestyle of danger and violence and once the war was over sought to perpetuate that thrill in the most exciting way available to them. Certainly, once Cromwell was dead and Charles II had been restored to the throne, many spoiled rich young men took to the road purely to assuage boredom, or to pay off gambling debts.

The restoration of the monarchy was the advent of the golden age of highway robbery. It was a time of licentiousness, and many colourful figures robbed the country blind with the tacit approval of the king and the adulation of the public. Highway robbers were the new folk heroes, universally lionised by everyone apart from their victims. Very few areas of the country seemed to be excluded from their influence and virtually no one, irrespective of position, was exempt from their attentions. Even as late as the mid-1700s, Prime Minister Robert Walpole's cheek was creased by a bullet from notorious highwayman James Macleane's gun, (although Macleane later claimed it was an accidental discharge).

Geographically some areas were more prone to highway robbery than others. Nottinghamshire was never particularly perceived to be one of these criminal black spots – that dubious distinction belonged to Buckinghamshire, Hertfordshire and the capital. Yet Nottingham's dealings with members of the highway-robbing class, who were either spawned on its streets or unlucky enough to cross its borders, exploded many of the stereotypes and preconceptions of what exactly constituted a highwayman.

When the Civil War was over, many veterans from the lower classes, brutalised and hardened by combat, began to pad out the ranks of the highwaymen. Nottingham man Richard Bracy was of the lower classes but not a war veteran. Martial conflict had not hardened in him a resolve toward violence – it didn't need to. Bracy's disposition was violent from an early age. He was a child thief who, as a teenager, was rumoured to have beaten a servant girl to death. By the time he had reached eighteen years of age, he had taken to highway robbery. Bracy gathered around himself a gang of eleven thugs who terrorised the highways of Newark, Nottingham and Derbyshire. He was a foul-tempered man with a predilection for torture and it was unusual for any of his robberies to be conducted without recourse to violence. He tied up a family in their farm house and forced them to reveal the whereabouts of £1,200 worth of plunder. He stole £1,800 from a coach and assaulted the driver. He took £600 from a Lady Jane Scoop, but not before attempting to rape her. His most appalling crime was the murder of a young boy believed to have overheard his gang making plans in a public house. Bracy killed the boy and buried him in a cellar.

Financially the gang's haul was astronomical for its time, but their reign was short. Bracy and his gang blighted the East Midlands' countryside for two years before they were caught and tried. It seemed fitting that for one who preyed on serving girls and pot boys, Bracy was betrayed by a servant. Lying in bed with his wife in a country hideout on the outskirts of Nottingham, Bracy woke to find himself surrounded by the officers of the law. Some accounts have him resisting violently and engaging in a brief gun battle. Others have him submitting to the authorities without a struggle.

Within three months of Bracy's arrest, his entire gang had been rounded up and imprisoned. Two of them (Richard Piggen and John Baker) turned on the rest and gave the authorities valuable and incriminating information. Richard Bracy was hanged. In an inversion of the highwayman's normal post-mortem glorification, Bracy was ignored by the balladeers. Fittingly his crimes were universally condemned by the same people who would have normally clamoured for any new information concerning the latest wicked deed of the most currently fashionable highwayman.

In 1766 two Nottingham highwaymen made a bid for consideration as the most eccentric or witty of their criminal class. James Bromage and William Wainer's exploits were average by dint of comparison with their contemporaries. Like Richard Bracy, both men were from the lower classes; Wainer was a framework knitter, Bromage a servant. They were childhood friends who, between them, robbed a Durham man and a Chester coach before their arrest and imprisonment. It was an underwhelming criminal legacy but Bromage and Wainer's claim for distinction came on the eve of their hanging. It was customary for the condemned to hear a final sermon before execution, in a last-ditch attempt to redeem the souls of men presumably destined for hellfire. In this instance, the sermon took place at St Mary's church on High Pavement. After the sermon had been preached, the men were to be hanged and their bodies returned to the church cemetery for burial. Bromage and Wainer insisted on first examining their graves before they departed, concerned that their corpses would not fit properly into the freshly dug holes. Both men climbed down into their own graves and tried them out for size. Satisfied that they would be suitably snug, Bromage and Wainer climbed out and boarded the cart that would take them to Gallows Hill.

The greatest highwayman ever associated with Nottingham was a woman. Joan Phillips was a farmer's daughter from Northamptonshire. Her upbringing was extremely respectable. She is believed to have been an exceptionally beautiful young woman and much sought after. Her family's wishes for her would have entailed a good marriage to someone of equivalent social standing. She fell in love with a clerk; Edward Bracey, the lower-class object of her affection, went through the proper channels to win Joan's hand in marriage but was unsuccessful. Edward asked Joan's father for permission to wed but was abruptly turned down. Joan's father may have had good cause to rebuff the clerk. *The Nottingham Date Book* cites Bracey as a charlatan from the off, faking 'a position in society which he did not occupy' in order to win Joan's hand in marriage.

The site of James Bromage and William Wainer's lodgings, formerly a public house, now part of the White Horse shopping arcade.

St Mary's cemetery, where Bromage and Wainer tried out their own graves for size prior to being executed.

Joan and Edward either eloped or else Joan was expelled from the family home by her angry father. The two lovers may have even robbed Joan's father before leaving. They fled to the north of the country, with Joan dressed in her lover's clothes, and sought refuge with John Bracey, a relative of Edward's. John Bracey was also known as William Bracey, as well as by his pseudonymous surname, Nevinson, and would become universally known by his nickname, 'Swift Nicks'. Swift Nicks Nevinson is second only to Dick Turpin as the most glorified highway robber in English criminal history.

In actuality, Nevinson's achievements far outstripped those of the frequently over-praised Dick Turpin (Nevinson's most spectacular exploit even being falsely attributed to Turpin). Swift Nicks conformed to every stereotypical notion of the romantic gentleman robber: he was born into money; he was a royalist; as a child he established an aptitude for crime, leading a gang of young thieves in his native Pontefract. He stole cutlery from his family, made away with his schoolmaster's horse and rode to London. Descriptions of the stolen horse would have been circulated. Association with the animal would have incriminated him, so he killed it. He sought employment with a brewer and then robbed him. He fled London for Europe and Flanders and, after a brief brush with the law, sought refuge in the army of the Duke of York. Returning to England, once his regiment had disbanded, Nevinson was reconciled with his parents and made good on the money that he had taken. With the fringe benefits of a military education to fortify him, Nevinson turned to highway robbery. He was ubiquitous, running protection rackets amongst the drovers in Yorkshire and robbing coaches in the South. It was at a notorious black spot in Kent that Nevinson graduated from the notorious to the mythic after robbing a man at gunpoint in Gad's Hill. The man must have recognised Nevinson, or his horse, or else Nevinson was an obvious suspect: in any event, prior to the robbery, Nevinson had recognised the need to establish an alibi. The robbery took place at four o'clock in the morning in Kent. By seven o'clock that evening, Nevinson was in York. He had ridden the entire distance on horseback. In all probability he used a host of horses stashed at various way stations, snatching half an hour's sleep here and a half hour's sleep there. How exactly he did it remains a source of debate but the fact that he did it is taken as gospel. By eight o'clock, Nevinson had changed his clothes and paraded himself in the presence of the Mayor of York, making certain that he asked him for the time of day. And so, when Nevinson was arrested for a highway robbery in Kent, he was able to produce the Mayor of York to verify his whereabouts 200 miles away.

Nevinson's deed attracted the attention of King Charles II, who summoned the highwayman to court. He promised him amnesty for the crime in question if he would only relate the story of how he established his seemingly miraculous alibi. Nevinson acquiesced to the king's demand. The king marvelled at Nevinson's speed and commented that the highwayman was swifter than Old Nick himself. The king had christened Nevinson with his most endearing moniker, but Dick Turpin stole his glory when posterity conferred the adventure onto him.

Joan Phillips and Edward Bracey had come under the protection of an authentic master criminal. They joined Nevinson's gang and flourished under his mentorship: Edward was even considered by many to be Swift Nicks' second-in-command. For her part, Joan carried on wearing men's clothing. She had even passed herself off as a man among Nevinson's followers, her true identity only known to her lover and Swift Nicks. The couple lived and robbed together. Joan took to the road armed with two pistols, dressed in male clothing. And although Joan and Edward never married, she took his name and was more commonly known as Joan Bracey than Joan Phillips. Between them, they plundered the roads around Yorkshire and Nottinghamshire.

At some point in their careers, 'the Braceys' ran a public house together in Bristol. Inevitably, the inn proved to be a magnet for the wastrel classes. This was ideal as far as the couple were concerned for, as well as those capable of navigating the treacherous currents of the underworld, the pub attracted the

Joan Phillips, one of the nation's most notorious female highway robbers.

odd arrogant dupe with delusions of criminal grandeur. These types of people were meat and drink to the Braceys and ripe for the taking. On one occasion Joan and Edward befriended Mr Rumbold, a rich young man of property. He accompanied them on a highway robbery only to be told that the couple would inform on him if he did not sign over land to them worth £100 a year. Mr Rumbold had no choice but to submit to their blackmail – it was either that or the gallows.

Another advantage of being a publican was the fact that Joan was not under any obligation to disguise her sex. No longer fettered by the need to don criminal drag, Joan began to attract attention all over again for her good looks.

In an age of unprecedented sexual license among the general populace, the ante was considerably upped amongst the outlaw classes. Highwaymen were known for their slew of mistresses, secret wives, lovers and litters of bastards, but Edward and Joan were conspicuous for their fidelity. That did not stop overconfident gentlemen occasionally trying their luck with the publican's wife when they thought her husband was away on business – and Edward and Joan were secure enough in each other's trust to happily exploit a prospective cuckold's boldness to their own financial advantage. One celebrated incident involved a Mr Dacey, who sexually propositioned Joan. Rather than rebuffing him, Joan encouraged Mr Dacey to come back and make good on his promises during the night when her husband was absent. Mr Dacey returned as instructed. He was encouraged by a complicit servant to strip to his nightshirt and enter Joan's bedroom. Stories vary as to what happened next. Some accounts had Mr Dacey entering Joan's bedroom only to be confronted with Edward Bracey armed with a sabre who proceeded to rob him. Other stories have Dacey entering Joan's darkened bedchamber to hear her disembodied voice enticing him to follow her. Believing it to be some form of elaborate foreplay, Dacey was led, in the dark, through various chambers and secret passages of the house, only to be dumped back onto the street minus his

The spot where Joan Phillips was hanged, on the junction between Wilford Lane and Loughborough Road.

clothes and money. Whichever of the two stories is true, (or whether either of them are true), the potent mythology of Edward and Joan's constancy to thievery and to one another was at once part of and at variance with the criminal landscape of Restoration England. It was only when the two thieves worked independently that things began to unravel.

Joan and Edward both died painful deaths in the same year – 1685. In 1684 Swift Nicks' empire had come crashing down around his ears when a landlady doped his drink and betrayed him to the authorities. He was tried and hanged in York. Joan Phillips' end came when she robbed a coach on the Loughborough road on the outskirts of Nottingham. It should have been a routine pinch but the victim took her by surprise when, rather than meekly capitulating, he rushed her and hit her so hard he knocked her off her horse, badly winding her. She was overpowered and delivered to the authorities. It was only when she had been formally arrested and detained in the County Gaol that her true gender was revealed. A female highway robber was a *cause célèbre* and during her trial, the county court was packed to the rafters with curious spectators. She was found guilty and sentenced to death by hanging. Her execution site is believed to have been at the point where Wilford Lane and Loughborough Road converge. It is also reckoned that Edward Bracey was present in the crowd and watched his common-law wife die. Joan Phillips' body was cut down and given over to friends to be buried.

Bracey's death occurred a scant six days later. He had stopped at an inn for a drink. It is ironic that Bracey was finally undone because he failed to observe one of the first lessons learnt by his mentor, Swift Nicks. Bracey died on account of his horse: he had been riding the same mount for far too long. His horse was recognised as the same animal that had been used in a recent highway robbery. It did not take a great deal of deduction to reason that the owner of the horse was more than likely a wanted man. As word of Bracey's true nature began to ripple through the public house, certain people began to arm themselves.

A loud blast sounded from the direction of the public house and Bracey's horse was shot and killed. Whether the shot came from a blunderbuss is not certain – it was a powerful discharge in any case and tore the fingers off both of Bracey's hands. A second blast came from a fowling piece, a powerful single-shot rifle used for hunting. Bracey was hit in the stomach. Somehow, on foot, he managed to elude the gunmen and found himself a place to hide.

It took him three days to die.

4

Malin Hill: the Theft of a Set of Curtains Spirals into Something a Little More Serious...

Linking the affluent area around High Pavement with the impoverished slums of Narrow Marsh was a slim cobbled walkway named Malin Hill. Acting as a virtual town and country planning metaphor for the gulf between rich and poor, Malin Hill begins at the base of the cliff that used to form one of the borders of Narrow Marsh and ends at the summit where the homes of people of property once towered above the rancid dwelling places of the needy. In 1800, somewhere between these two geographical markers, a barber named George Caunt engaged in a stand-off with the law that would claim two lives.

Caunt's crime was theft. A resident of St James' Street, Caunt had stolen a set of curtains from a dancing master. The dancing master reported Caunt to the authorities, who issued a warrant for his arrest. When the local constable came looking for Caunt to serve his warrant, Caunt fled and took refuge at a friend's home in Malin Hill. The constable knew exactly where Caunt had gone to hide. He did not tackle Caunt directly but employed two more officers to wait at either end of the hill. Whether the constables were engaged in an overt blockade, or were employed in a Georgian variation on the modern stakeout, is uncertain. What is clear is that Caunt knew that they were there and was determined to evade capture. To begin with he simply waited. Caunt entered his hiding place on a Tuesday. By the time Saturday came around, he was still there. Four days in a state of virtual siege had exerted terrible pressure on Caunt's judgement – pressure that would fatally cloud his sense of perspective. George Caunt had stolen a set of curtains. In 1800 there were in excess of 200 offences that carried the death penalty – it was possibly the worst time in English legal history to be an incompetent thief. Nevertheless, the death penalty was only ever really invoked for approximately twenty crimes, transportation being a popular alternative among the judiciary. Of the previous four people to have been executed in Nottingham at that time, one had been for murder, one had been for rape, another had been for the theft of three cows, and the last had been for forgery. In all probability, Caunt stood a good chance of escaping the gallows. But what Caunt did next ensured that if he was caught and convicted, a hanging sentence would be inevitable.

George Caunt eventually emerged from his hiding place on Saturday armed with a horse pistol. Of all handguns of the period, the horse pistol was one of the most powerful. It was a foot long and designed for use by cavalry officers. At close quarters, the damage it could do would have been devastating. Caunt was approached by George Ball, one of the three constables. Caunt shot him dead and evaded the two remaining officers. Ball's body was taken to the Town Hall. The following day a coroner pronounced a verdict of wilful murder. A manhunt began in earnest.

Right: Malin Hill.

Below: Hapless murderer George Caunt tries to stab himself in the heart. It was to be his second botched suicide attempt.

The former site of the suicide cemetery at the top of Derby Road. George Caunt's body was buried here by the authorities but later exhumed by his friends.

George Caunt made it as far as the village of Alfreton on the outskirts of Nottingham. He shut himself in a room, took a phial of poison and began to drink it. But Caunt couldn't even kill himself properly; the authorities burst into his room and wrested the phial from his mouth. He was escorted back to Nottingham. Caunt made a second attempt on his own life when his captors stopped at an inn for something to eat. Caunt took advantage of the sudden presence of sharp cutlery and tried to stab himself in the heart. He missed and hit his breastbone.

It was only when he was placed in gaol that the poison that he had managed to ingest began to take effect. It took him two days to die. The coroners were called upon once again. They pronounced a verdict of *felo de se*, or self-murder. Suicide was a crime punishable by confiscation of property and/or shameful burial (unless the perpetrator was a child or of unsound mind). The authorities left Caunt's property alone but buried him at the Sandhills suicide plot at the top of Derby Road. It was customary to bury a suicide at night without a coffin or any religious ceremony. By the standards of the time, this was a highly dishonourable interment.

If dignity had eluded George Caunt in his lifetime, then his friends endeavoured to provide him with a little in death. They failed. Having dug Caunt up, they sought a proper burial place for him. In hindsight, one suspects that they might have preferred to have found a suitable resting place before exhuming Caunt's corpse. It took them a couple of days before they were able to secure a desirable plot. In the meantime, Caunt's friends were obliged to lug his body around with them almost everywhere they went.

Eventually, George Caunt was reburied in the General Baptist burial ground on Stoney Street, just around the corner from Malin Hill.

5

The Terror of an Example: the Terminal Aftermath of a Public Execution

Public hanging had been an accepted form of capital punishment in England since Saxon times and in its application Nottingham was no different from any other town or city in the country. Initially a punishment reserved for traitors (King John strung twenty-eight teenaged hostages from the battlements of Nottingham Castle in 1280), hanging soon became the common punishment for murderers and thieves. By the eighteenth century, 200 separate offences carried the death penalty. By the nineteenth century, criminals were routinely hanged on collapsing gallows by professional hangmen rather than from trees, but the results were essentially the same – death by strangulation.

At various times during the nineteenth century, there were four main locations where criminals might be hanged in Nottingham: the House of Correction, Bagthorpe Gaol, Gallows Hill and the front steps of the Shire Hall. Until the 1830s, most public executions took place on Gallows Hill. The hill's exact location is unknown. A best guess places it at the top of Mansfield Road where St Andrew's church is currently located, or else directly opposite on the site of the cemetery at the junction between Mansfield Road and Forest Road.

After Gallows Hill had been rejected as the town's foremost execution site, Nottingham's preferred location became the Shire Hall. By this time, many of the parasitic gallows traditions were being phased out: medical dissection of the condemned had been outlawed[2], as had the use of the gibbet to display their bodies (which, by law now, had to be buried within the grounds of the gaol). Capital offences had been reduced from 200 to a handful and debates raged among the intelligentsia about the overall effectiveness of public execution. There was a slow crawl toward reform. But it was in this climate of relative moral amendment that Nottingham distinguished itself in infamy. On 7 August 1844, during a public execution, something happened that killed more spectators than were ever actually hanged on the steps of the Shire Hall. Nottingham

---

2. Once the execution had taken place the body might be cut down and returned to the court house. In the same room where the death sentence had been passed, the body would be dissected for the purposes of medical instruction. The doors of the court room would be thrown open and the same public that had watched the condemned die would parade in front of the eviscerated corpse. When the surgeons and the public had had their fun, the cadaver might then be hoisted in a gibbet and displayed on a roadside as a lesson to all potential law breakers.

Above left: The execution of William Saville on the steps of the Shire Hall.

Above right: The cemetery at the top of Mansfield Road is believed to be one of the two possible locations of Gallows Hill, the site where the majority of Nottingham's public executions were carried out.

St Andrew's church, another likely location for Gallows Hill.

A dirt path in Colwick Woods, where William Saville committed his brutal quadruple murder.

had joined the referendum on capital punishment in earnest and the man at the centre of a storm of controversy was a murderer named William Saville.

William Saville was born in Arnold in 1815. He spent his childhood in Blidworth, where he dabbled in farming, eventually earning his livelihood as a framework knitter. When Saville was in his twenties, he met Ann Ward. She was older than he was and unmarried with an illegitimate child. Saville and Ward slept together and Ward became pregnant. Saville was disinclined to wed but Ward's sister compelled William to marry with the offer of money. William accepted. Although the married couple produced another two children between them, it was not a happy union. Nevertheless they stayed together for a staggering nine years before Saville determined that he had had enough. In January 1844 William Saville left his wife and family. He had made no financial provision for them and they had no choice but to enter the poorhouse. Saville, on the other hand, had met a lady and was trying his luck in a different part of town. Before long, William Saville had made plans to emigrate to America and remarry. The fact that Saville had neglected to divorce his first wife didn't appear to trouble him in the slightest. Nor did he feel the need to inform his prospective bride that he was already wed. Ann Saville eventually tracked her husband down and shamed him into returning home.

On 31 May 1844, William Saville took his wife and children for a walk in Colwick Woods. The family were spotted at twenty-five minutes past twelve in the afternoon. Saville was seen alone at half past twelve. In the space of five minutes (in the stretch of land currently located between Greenwood Road and Colwick Road), William Saville had murdered his entire family. Producing a razor, he slit their throats and arranged the corpses to look like Ann had killed her own children before turning the blade on herself. When Saville had finished he returned home and made himself something to eat. The bodies were discovered two hours later. William Saville was arrested and charged with murder.

The Shire Hall, the execution site of William Saville, now the location of the Galleries of Justice, a museum of crime and punishment.

Saville's crime, horrific as it was, was entirely consistent with the criminal spirit of the age on two counts: firstly, his principle target was a woman. Of the twenty-five murders resulting in a conviction that passed through Nottingham's courts during the reign of Queen Victoria, nineteen of the victims were female. Secondly, his choice of weapon was the cut-throat razor. Of the fifty-nine executions that took place in Nottingham over the course of the nineteenth century, eight of the murderers hanged had used cut-throat razors to kill their victims. In a pre-forensic era, when virtually every gentleman owned a razor and carried it about on his person, it was the obvious thing to reach for in the height of passion or premeditation. The cut-throat razor would become one of the most frequently used murder weapons of the period.

Saville's trail was swift. Yet even by the elastic standards of the mid-nineteenth century, the case against him wasn't exactly perceived as airtight. He clearly had the motive for murder but the evidence against him was largely circumstantial. All he had to do was to keep his composure and deny everything and he stood a fair chance of being acquitted. Bizarrely enough, it was William Saville who sealed his own fate. For reasons that are still not entirely certain, Saville confessed his crime to Henry Freeman, a soldier with whom he was sharing a gaol cell. Henry Freeman informed on him. On 27 July 1844, William Saville stood trial for murder.

The most sensationalistic accounts of Saville's trial can be found in the broadsheets circulated around the time of the hanging. Best understood as a fusion of tabloid newspaper and sporting programme, broadsheets were one of the many industries that thrived during public hangings. They contained salacious accounts of the condemned's evil deeds, complete with transcripts (often entirely made-up) of the guilty party's final confession. As historical sources they are highly dubious, their agenda being entertainment rather than reportage, the more sensationalistic the better, but according to a broadsheet circulated at the time, Saville stated that he was, 'well satisfied with the manner in which his defence was conducted', claiming that he 'could have brought witnesses to disprove much of the evidence' but simply chose not to. It was a bizarre pronouncement, possibly invented by the broadsheet's anonymous author, but admittedly consistent with Saville's imprudent confession and seeming obliviousness to the consequences of his actions. Saville was found guilty and sentenced to death.

The normal ritual for most people convicted of a capital offence was to spend anything between two to three weeks in confinement. This was considered a suitable amount of time for any evidence to be produced that might overturn the guilty verdict. It was also a time for religious contemplation and hopefully repentance on the part of the guilty party, helped to a penitent point of view by frequent visits from a clergyman appropriate to their religion. The final two weeks would be spent in the dark, solitary condemned cells every gaol was equipped with. A special sermon might be preached on the eve of a hanging (normally a Sunday anyhow), tailored to the fate of the condemned. A hangman had to be sent for. Outside of London, gaols did not generally employ resident executioners. Every region in the kingdom had its share of itinerant hangmen who would travel to the appropriate gaol at short notice with an assistant or an apprentice in tow.

On the morning of the hanging the condemned would rise before seven. They were entitled to have a meal if they could stomach it and were offered the sacrament. Around about eight o'clock they would be led to the gallows somewhere outside of the prison, accompanied by wardens, the governor and the clergy. They would be taken to the gallows and placed over a trapdoor. The condemned's arms and legs would be pinioned by the hangman. The condemned would have the opportunity to say something to the crowd before a white hood was placed over their face and the noose around their neck. The hangman would pull the lever and the condemned would fall through the trapdoor. In the age of public hanging, death was painful and protracted. The long drop technique that would break the neck and kill a person inside of a minute had yet to be refined. A shortened rope was customary and would ensure death by asphyxiation. It could take anything up to fifteen minutes to die.

On 7 August at half past eight in the morning, William Saville was led out onto the scaffold that had been erected on the steps of the Shire Hall. He was to be executed in full view of the mammoth crowd that was crammed into the narrow confines of High Pavement.

The crowd were an essential element in a hanging. To kill a man in front of his peers was considered a deterrent to future wrongdoing for any potential or active law breaker present in the mob. Many an evangelist would take advantage of the large numbers of people that flocked to public hangings and harangue them with talk of heaven and hell. But the crowd were often drunk. Hangings attracted prostitutes; pickpockets worked the crowds of spectators and pie sellers did sterling business.[3] There were brawls. Publicans lucky enough to be situated within easy view of the gallows would rent rooms out to the wealthy or respectable. These rooms would serve in much the same capacity as a balcony seat at a theatre. Hangmen exploited their position by selling souvenirs of the occasion. These could be the personal effects of the condemned, or pieces of the hangman's rope. Children flocked to hangings. When the condemned was finally executed, there would often be a moment of quiet immediately afterward that could be interpreted as some kind of religious solemnity, but it would invariably be followed by laughing, shouting and coarse joking. One would have to look very hard to find any evidence of moral edification amongst the spectators of the average public execution.

---

3. William Calcraft, the longest ever serving English hangman, originally sold pies at Newgate Prison and Horsemonger Lane – London's most popular execution sites.

A rooftop view of High Pavement, seen from the Shire Hall. The narrow area below was packed with spectators keen to see William Saville hang. Many in the crowd were crushed to death in the appalling disturbance immediately after the execution.

There were less than thirty-five feet between the frontage of the Shire Hall, where Saville's Gallows had been erected, and the buildings on the other side of the road. The space in between was packed with spectators. When Saville was hanged two things seemed to happen at once: those nearest to the scaffold recoiled and those at the back pushed forward to get a better view. The crowd became agitated and started to jostle. Panic began to take hold of the assembly and people started to search for places of safety. There was nowhere to go. Sections of the crowd were crushed against the walls opposite the gallows. The pressure mounted, becoming so immense that the front door of a local surgeon's house imploded and spectators tumbled into his home. He immediately began to treat the injured. Others were less fortunate.

Many people raced toward Garners Hill, a narrow path that connected High Pavement with the slum of Narrow Marsh below. People tripped and fell and bodies began to pile up on top of one other. Throughout the length and breadth of High Pavement and in the bottleneck at Garners Hill, people were dying and terrible injuries were being sustained. Twelve were killed in the crush; five more would die later. Scores more had sustained serious wounds. Of the dead, eight of them were under fifteen years of age.

Much of the worst of the disaster was observed by the Mayor of Nottingham from the vantage point of his lodging window opposite the Shire Hall. He behaved with distinction during the disaster, almost throwing himself out of the window in an attempt to stay the catastrophe. He also opened his lodgings to the public in order to treat the injured.

The mayor was deeply troubled by what he had seen and immediately wrote a letter to the Home Office, sharply criticising the choice of High Pavement as a location for any further hangings. He blamed the disaster on a mixture of Derby pickpockets and 'mischievous persons throwing hats and shoes' that had excited and agitated the crowd.

The Home Office responded. Mr Enfield, the Under Sheriff of Nottingham, was given the responsibility of investigating. He gave the matter some thought and reported back to London suggesting an alternative to High Pavement. He reasoned that the Debtors Yard in the County Gaol would be a suitable location for any future hangings. The County Gaol was located directly beneath the Shire Hall, cut into the sandstone cliff face that overlooked Narrow Marsh. The Debtors Yard was partially visible from outside to some, if not all, of the surrounding area. This was deemed a suitable compromise by Enfield, ensuring a degree of visibility, as well as complete safety for the public. Enfield's report reached the Home Secretary on 14 August.

Three days later, a gathering of Nottingham magistrates conferred. They rejected the Under Sheriff's suggestion on the basis that the Debtors Yard was simply not public enough. Public safety was important but the issue at stake was one of moral example: it wasn't enough for the public to see the body fall through the trap door from a distance. They had to see the condemned man's face before the hood was placed over it. They had to be able to hear any words of repentance from the condemned man's lips. The Home Secretary was in complete concurrence. He gave the magistrates the full weight of his moral support, insisting that the point of public execution was 'the terror of the example'.

The practical solution and the implications of the magistrates' decision would have to wait for a while as it would be sixteen years before anybody in Nottingham would do anything appalling enough to warrant execution. In 1860 John Fenton, a thirty-seven-year-old blacksmith and publican, committed murder. His execution would take place on High Pavement as decreed, but this time, extensive measures were taken to ensure the public's safety. Architect Richard Charles Sutton was commissioned to render the area safe for spectators so that they could appreciate the execution without fear of serious injury. Sutton was given a free hand to do what he saw fit. At a cost of £80 he set up a series of interconnecting zigzagging barriers that broke up the crowd. Sutton placed the barriers in front of the Shire Hall, at Weekday Cross at the bottom of High Pavement, and at Garners Hill where the greatest loss of life had occurred. He ensured that High Pavement was cleared the night before and that nobody was permitted to enter the street until six o'clock the following morning. To ensure that order was kept the area was supervised by up to 130 police officers from the county and borough forces. Ironically, Sutton disapproved of public hangings, calling them 'wretched and demoralising exhibitions'.

John Fenton was hanged without any bother on the same gallows that had been used to execute three Reform Bill rioters in 1832. Fewer people attended the hanging than had been present at the William Saville execution and nobody was injured. The only sniff of trouble came from the disgruntled moaning of warehouse workers who had been forbidden from using High Pavement the night before.

There was only one more public hanging in Nottingham before the law changed. In 1868 public hanging was outlawed altogether and all executions were moved into the interior of Nottingham's prisons. It had been a legal struggle that had transfixed the nation and Nottingham had played its part in the furious national debate over whether or not it was moral to hang a criminal in public. But what is striking about the whole affair is that, throughout the discourse that had polarised opinion up and down the country, even amongst the most progressive critics of capital punishment, the question of whether the death penalty should have been completely abolished was hardly ever raised.

6

A Disorderly Radical City: a Brief History of Rioting in Nottingham

The single most catastrophic riots in English history were the Gordon Riots of 1780. In a week of violence (in protest against the repeal of long-standing anti-Catholic legislation) a gigantic mob ripped London to pieces. Parliament was besieged. Newgate Prison was torched and emptied of its convict population. Lambeth Palace and the headquarters of the Bow Street Runners were attacked. Law and order collapsed. Stability was only restored once the king had unofficially ordered the military to act independently of the magistrates. Once the riot had been quelled the death toll was estimated at anything between 800 and 1,000 people. Whilst the levels of violence displayed in the Gordon Riots were unprecedented, rioting itself was an all too regular occurrence in the industrial towns and cities of England in the eighteenth and nineteenth centuries. The most persistent and notorious offender was Nottingham.

Nottingham had been subject to smatterings of civil disorder throughout its history. In the fifteenth century, Yorkist veterans of the Wars of the Roses terrorised the town and subjected local government officials to a barrage of arrows for having had the temerity to support the wrong side during the conflict. Two people were killed in the commotion. It was an undoubtedly dramatic event in the history of Nottingham, but it was an atypical occurrence, and no better and no worse than any of the numerous post-war disturbances plaguing towns up and down the country. Yet by the end of the nineteenth century, Nottingham's bad reputation was synonymous with rioting.

The Food Riots of the 1750s and '60s were the first real flowerings of Nottingham's seditious reputation. During this period the poor were at the mercy of dramatically fluctuating food prices. Often these were determined by bad harvests, the inevitable consequences of a mainly rural economy. But in many instances workers were flagrantly held to ransom by greedy traders bolstered by a legislature that offered little support for the starving underclass. In these circumstances, riots were an inevitability.

In 1756, three colliers were arrested for their part in a march on Nottingham in protest against inflated food prices. The rest of the marchers took immediate offence and intimidated the mayor into letting the colliers go. Not satisfied with that, the crowd went on to smash a local mill to pieces. This set the precedent for subsequent Nottingham riots. In the next half-century every food group seemed to have at least one corresponding riot associated with it. Nottingham rioted over butter in 1785 and meat in 1786. Meat was the cause of another riot in 1799 during which Nottingham butcher's stalls were looted and then set on fire. In 1766 Nottingham rioted over

Rival gangs clash in the Market Place during the 1865 general election.

the price of cheese, going so far as to use large heavy blocks as projectiles during the fighting. By 1800 the mob had come full circle and were rioting over the price of grain once more with renewed assaults on their old enemies, the millers.

The advent of the Napoleonic Wars signalled the close of Nottingham's first golden age of rioting. The name of Nottingham had become so linked with rioting that the town became the location for the country's first provincial military barracks. As well as being a practical measure (given Nottingham's volatility) it was also a pre-emptive bid to nip a potential national revolution in the bud. The government and the monarchy were understandably paranoid about the probability of a full-scale French invasion at the time. They were equally frightened of the prospect of a Gallic-style revolt erupting on home soil. Nottingham was forefront amongst candidates for the town most likely to incubate revolutionary tendencies. Yet the war years were relatively quiet in the East Midlands. Nottingham was politically anti-war initially, but after a lull in hostilities (and certainly once the war had resumed in 1803) the town did an about-face and became staunchly patriotic.

Towards the end of the war years, industrialists were subject to a more insidious threat. The liberal use of framework-knitting machines in the hosiery trade resulted in the mass production of cheaper goods and inevitable sackings and lowering of wages. Skilled tradesmen were put out of business and many workers faced the prospect of starvation. There was the predictable eruption of frame-breaking riots, coupled with the emergence of organisations such as the Luddite movement. For a spell, the Nottingham factory owners' fear of masked Luddites breaking their machines and murdering them in their living rooms supplanted that of the mob.

In 1811 Luddite Daniel Diggle was hanged on the steps of the Shire Hall for his part in the attempted murder of factory owner George Kerry. The Luddite problem was seen as so subversive by the capital that two magistrates were sent up from London to deal with the problem and swear in special constables.

Although the establishment were threatened enough to introduce the death sentence for machine breaking, the Luddite outrage was short-lived. Their reign of terror lasted a scant five years. It was a strange, covert revolutionary anomaly not really consistent with Nottingham's criminal character. So, in 1831, the old ways were resumed with a vengeance and the time-honoured tactic of smashing a town to pieces to register collective disapproval started all over again. The touch fire for the next wave of violence was the rejection of the Reform Bill in the House of Lords.

The Reform Bill of 1831 was a piece of legislation designed to award greater voting rights to the labouring classes. Nottingham was politically pro-reform in its municipal government but also home to a powerful minority of land owners steadfastly against the Bill. Chief amongst them was the Duke of Newcastle. It was on Newcastle's estate near the castle (a property that he also owned) that the Nottingham barracks had been situated. Newcastle was outspoken regarding the Bill. As a consequence of his opinions, the windows of his London residence had been smashed earlier during the year.

The Reform Bill was passed in the House of Commons. On 2 October 1831 it was debated in the House of Lords. Chief among the Bill's opponents was the Duke of Newcastle himself. The Lords rejected the Bill and the bad news began to filter through to the provinces. The Lords' decision reached Nottingham by 8 October. The annual Goose Fair was in full flow in the town's Market Place. Spirits were high at this time of year anyway and the news of the Reform Bill's decline stoked an already giddy mix of heightened emotions. Soldiers were warned to expect trouble.

The initial demonstrations were peaceful enough, but concurrent to the lawful demonstrators, a mob was beginning to form. When the storm clouds broke in earnest, the rioters targeted many of the landowners who had been conspicuous in their opposition to the Bill. The mob tried to burn down the Colwick residence of an anti-Reform Bill magistrate. They attempted to storm the House of Correction. The governor of the County Gaol even swore he heard rioters at the base of the gaol's wall, plotting to prime the sandstone caves of Narrow Marsh with gunpowder and blast the gaol open.

Having been only partially successful in their objectives, the mob were to excel themselves with their next target. On 11 October they turned their attention to the Duke of Newcastle and Nottingham Castle itself. Mercifully, Newcastle was out of Nottingham at the time his Midlands home was overrun and burned to ashes. And such was the hatred reserved for the duke that when the flames had died down sufficiently, the mob returned to the castle and demolished its charred ruins.

The rioters also managed to burn down a silk factory in Beeston on the outskirts of Nottingham. They looted property and terrorised individuals between Nottingham and Beeston. The soldiers who had been prudently stationed, but had proved shamefully impotent during the bulk of the rioting, eventually managed to restore order to the town, the militia saving Wollaton Hall from arson.

In the aftermath of the riots, there were many arrests but few serious convictions. Yet many of those who were convicted were treated as harshly as the law allowed. Three men were hanged on the steps of the Shire Hall and four were transported to the colonies. The convictions were unpopular and support for reform was resolute.[4]

---

4. After the formation of the first Metropolitan Police Force in 1829, resistance to the idea of policing the provinces was rife amongst local government. It took until 1856 for the policing of all boroughs and counties to become compulsory. Yet Nottingham was amongst the first towns in England to embrace the London model. The catastrophe of the Reform Bill Riots was the catalyst for this decision.

Eight months after the riots, the Reform Bill was eventually passed. The Reform Act was a disappointment. Voting rights were granted to any man who owned property worth £10 or more, but this was a paltry concession that still excluded the majority of the male populace. Resentment began to simmer all over again and the foundations were laid for a fresh season of rioting.

The next phase of civil disorder would be different in character. Riots would no longer be spontaneous eruptions of working-class frustration; they would be organised. Disciplined criminal elements would be a more manifest ingredient and riots would be underpinned by a more cohesive political ideology. Also, the riots would draw in members from all social classes. No longer would the battle lines be drawn on economic and social grounds. Instead, the architects of these riots would be landowners themselves pitting their own private armies against one another.

The lawful reaction to the compromises of the First Reform Act was Chartism. The People's Charter was drafted to perpetuate a radical overhaul of the voting system. Amongst the reforms called for, the charter demanded universal male suffrage and an end to property determining who could or could not vote. Petitions were delivered to Parliament and mass demonstrations were the order of the day. Nottingham was Chartist to its boots and a centre of much activity. The Market Place and the open leisure spaces of the Forest were frequently packed with Chartist demonstrators. As the Chartist movement gathered momentum in the East Midlands, the authorities initially expected trouble. But by and large (in Nottingham at any rate), the late 1830s were relatively peaceful. The 1840s would be different.

In April 1841, Napoleonic war veteran and MP for Nottingham, Major General Sir Robert Ferguson, died. A by-election was called. A Mr John Walters for the Conservative Party and a Mr Larpent for the Liberals stood against one another. Violence and bribery were rife during the campaign. Each candidate slandered the other in specially published sheets. John Walters won the election. In June of the following year a general election was called. The Tories fielded Thomas B. Charlton and John Walters. The Liberal Whigs put forward Sir J.C. Hobhouse in addition to Larpent. The Tories and the Liberals took turns leading processions into the town centre. Both sets of politicians addressed their supporters from the upper floors of public houses: the White Lion Pub for the Whigs, and the George IV for the Tories. Both parties sought the aid of the Nottingham Lambs, an organised gang of local thugs.

The Lambs had a criminal mythology dating back to the Napoleonic Wars. They were originally thought to have been soldiers of the Second Battalion of the 45th Sherwood Foresters. Whether this was true or not, the Lambs certainly structured themselves along military lines. The two areas of criminal endeavour where the Lambs excelled themselves were the illegal bare-knuckle prize fighting game and electioneering. Both pursuits highlighted two disparate elements of the Lambs' criminal character. When it came to prize fighting, the Lambs were deeply partisan. Chief Lambs were among many of the finest boxers of the era. William 'Bendigo' Thompson, the champion of England, was incontestably a member of the Lambs and believed by many to have been their leader. Lambs followed their boxers from fight to fight, intimidating officials and provoking some of the most outrageous ringside brawls in British boxing history. But as far as election rigging was concerned, the Lambs were utterly mercenary. They were apolitical and would happily hire themselves out to whoever offered them the most money. In the 1842 General Election both sides employed retinues of Lambs to protect their interests and steer the electorate to vote in their favour. It was estimated in Nottingham that the Tories and the Whigs had a hundred Lambs apiece at their disposal.

In the early stages of the election, Lamb tactics consisted of kidnapping voters and strategic acts of theft and vandalism. On 28 June, a gang of Whig Lambs attacked Tory supporters on

The open spaces of the old Market Place provided rioters with a natural arena in which to clash with the authorities. (Picture courtesy of Nottingham City Council and www.picturethepast.org.uk)

The former Market Place (now known as the Market Square), as it is today.

Mapperley Plains where thousands of Chartist demonstrators were confronted by soldiers on horseback.

Smithy Row near the Market Place. Many of the Lambs had bought their signature weapons with them – wooden clubs they affectionately called their 'twigs'. Both sides carried stones wrapped in the colours of their chosen political party – blue for Tory, yellow for Whig – and tried to hit each other with them. The Tories took a terrible beating and were forced to give ground. More Tories arrived on horseback armed with sticks and waded into the Whigs. The Whigs responded by trying to prise the stones out of the ground to throw them at the mounted reinforcements. The battle raged on until the army arrived and cleared the area.

Violence continued to erupt over the voting period. The Liberal Committee room was ransacked and the police were besieged. Only soldiers seemed able to keep order. Somehow, in the middle of all the chaos, the ballots of those who had actually managed to duck flying stones and evade the kidnap gangs were counted. The Whigs were victorious in Nottingham but the overall victory went to the Tories.

In 1842 the Chartists were out in force attempting to organise a national strike. In August, 2,000 Chartists assembled in Nottingham's Market Place. Magistrates and police attempted to move them on. Many demonstrators left the Market Place and regrouped up the road in Hockley. The police followed them and the atmosphere was electric with the expectation of violence. The Riot Act was read and the Chartists dispersed, only to reappear in Carrington and attempt to halt production in the local factories. The Riot Act was read once again. This proved to be an oft-repeated pattern of behaviour between the Chartists and the authorities, with increasingly brazen demonstrators popping up around the town and surrounding area only to be intercepted by the police, or the army when the crowds were too much for the police to cope with. Chartists were arrested and even chased across fields by mounted soldiers, yet all the while the anticipated riot did not occur. Eventually the Chartists left the town. They gathered in their thousands in the fields of the Mapperley Plains outside of Nottingham. An informant tipped off the authorities and the army were deployed. When the soldiers arrived the crowd were going peacefully about their business, eating tea on the grass. The Riot Act was read for the umpteenth time and the crowd were ordered to leave the fields. They refused and 400 were arrested, bound and marched in lines of four to the House of Correction. Of these, 250 were released within hours of their arrest; fifty demonstrators were forced to pay £5 to keep the peace for a year and twenty-four were given hard labour. Aside from a little stone throwing and a hairy moment when it looked like the army were about to open fire on the crowd, the events of August were not as combustive as initially feared. Nevertheless, the incident was referred to thereafter as the Battle of Mapperley Plains.

Despite small pockets of violence whenever there was an election, things were relatively quiet in Nottingham from that point until the 1860s. The arrival on the political scene of Sir Robert Clifton pushed organised electoral violence to new levels of outrage. The Eton-educated Clifton was politically a Liberal, albeit extreme, and popular amongst the Chartists. He was young and likeable. Having spent a lot of time in Paris, Clifton was considered exotic. He was a gifted and witty orator. He was also one of the most blatantly Machiavellian politicians in Nottingham's political history.

Prior to the advent of Clifton the most dominant and controversial figure on Nottingham's political landscape was Fergus O'Connor. Throughout the 1840s O'Connor was easily the most colourful and influential figure of the Chartist movement. He was an Irishman, a gifted speaker and something of hero in Nottingham who eventually earned the distinction of being the first chartist MP. He was a spirited man, not above occasionally settling a political disagreement with his fists, but essentially law abiding. When he died, passionate argument erupted over whether a vaunted commemorative statue was appropriate for such an allegedly disreputable rabble-rouser. In the context of this book, O'Connor is only worth mentioning because, although essentially conducting his political battles within the framework of the law, he was regarded among many as something of a villain, in spite of adequate evidence to the contrary. Sir Robert Clifton, on the other hand, was the genuine article.

Left: The speaker's platform is set ablaze by Sir Robert Clifton's supporters.

Far left: A statue of Sir Robert Clifton, one of the era's most flagrantly corrupt politicians.

Opposite: Mounted soldiers occupy the Market Place. Hussars were regularly employed to deal with rioters when the police proved themselves unequal to the task. (Picture courtesy of Nottingham Historical Film Unit and www.picturethepast.org.uk)

In the 1861 by-election Clifton stood against the Earl of Lincoln, who was the son of the reviled Duke of Newcastle. The gutted ruins of the castle remained a visible reminder of the part Lincoln's father had played in denying the working classes their electoral due. It was always going to be an uphill struggle for Lincoln to prevail against Clifton. But Clifton wasn't satisfied with submitting his considerable natural advantages to the machinery of democracy. He chose to cement his position with intimidation tactics. Before long the gangs were back on the streets, threatening those who chose to vote against Clifton.

Clifton won but there were minor consequences. He was rejected by his party who decided not to permit him to run in the 1865 general election. Undaunted, Clifton stood anyway, on an extreme Liberal ticket this time. The other candidates were Samuel Morley and Charles Paget, both traditional Liberals. Clifton was a better public speaker than either of them, subjecting both to a ruthless campaign of public ridicule.

In the Market Place, before a crowd of 15,000, Clifton insulted Morley and ridiculed the politician's stance on the consumption of alcohol. Morley was a dyed-in-the-wool temperance man. It was a position that should have made Morley look morally resolute in the face of Clifton's questionable character, but Morley's morals were a veritable gift to Clifton, who made him look like an inveterate killjoy to the thousands who had come to hear him speak. Clifton also had the nerve to accuse both of his rivals of hiring gangs of Lambs, despite the well-known fact that he kept very public company with the infamous Nottingham gang himself. Although the public name-calling was ugly, it was very much the nature of the beast in nineteenth-century politics. Besides, Morley and Paget would get their chance to address the crowds and say something equally derogatory about Clifton in exactly the same location... except Clifton had no intention of allowing that to happen.

Clifton had addressed his supporters in May. In June, a wooden platform was erected at the Market Place for Morley and Paget to hold their rally. Supporters from all over the country arrived in Nottingham by train, eager to hear their men speak. Clifton had deployed a gang of Lambs to meet them at the station. Morley and Paget's followers were viciously pelted with stones. Over the course of the next quarter of an hour, the victims of the barrage fought their way to the Market Place. En route they acquired some stones of their own and proceeded to throw them back at

the Lambs. Paget and Morley's men held the square for a while but were eventually forced away from the speaker's platform. The platform was torched by Clifton's Lambs. Morley and Paget's committee rooms were smashed up. Some even claimed that Clifton himself was present, egging his Lambs on to acts of further vandalism. The fighting continued throughout the night. Troops were summoned and the police eventually brought things to a belated conclusion with a baton charge. Approximately fifty people were injured in the violence; miraculously nobody was killed. Of the hundreds who must have taken part, only twenty-one men stood before the magistrates. No hefty sentences were handed down. The majority were simply bound over to keep the peace.

On 12 July, Morley and Clifton were declared the election winners. Although few people would suffer too severely under the law, the fallout from the riots did demand recompense in other ways. Chief Constable Hoddinton was forced to resign over his mishandling of the chaos, and in early 1866 petitions were sent to Parliament demanding that Clifton and Morley be stripped of their Member of Parliament status. A Commons committee deliberated for twenty-seven days before deciding that both men were 'not duly elected.' The election was pronounced void. Morley and Paget were declared guilty of bribery and Clifton's agents accused of bribery in the form of outrageous expenses awarded to voters who had to travel in to Nottingham. Clifton was deemed responsible for exerting 'undue influence by himself and others on his behalf' over the result of the election. It was a politely euphemistic way of saying that Clifton had hired a private army and turned the centre of Nottingham into a battlefield.

In spite of (or perhaps because of) all of this, Sir Robert Clifton remained popular throughout his life. When he died aged only forty-two years many Nottingham shop keepers shut up shop out of respect. Tens of thousands made a pilgrimage to his estate and his funeral was attended by 'an immense concourse of spectators'.

Rioting in Nottingham did not die out with Sir Robert Clifton. Even as the subsequent parliamentary reform acts incorporated all but one of the points of the People's Charter, elections were constantly beset by disturbances of one form or another. Throughout the reign of Queen Victoria, until 1880, there was not a single election in Nottingham that was unmarked by violence. As the century drew to a close, Nottingham had fully earned the rebuke of Sir Robert Peel who, as far back as 1835, had called her a 'disorderly, radical city'.

7

Manly Conduct: a Nottingham Prize-Fighter, his Esteemed Mentor and Brutal Rivals

On 4 May 1835 on the outskirts of Nottingham, two men met on Mapperley Plains to box one another for the right to woo a servant girl. The lady in question could not decide on which of the two men she wanted and determined that only the winner of the fight would be her lover. The contest lasted two hours. According to *The Nottingham Date Book*, the loser was battered 'insensible and died soon after.'

In 1867 the Marquis of Queensbury introduced a set of sporting rules that tamed, formalised and made respectable the previously illegal sport that had defined British notions of masculinity for over a century and a half. His insistence on padded gloves and the three-minute round signalled the official death knell of the bare-knuckle prize fight. But in fact, the preceding decade had already marked the final spasm of outlaw sporting excellence, with Nottingham playing its part as both hero and villain.

The Georgian and Victorian prize fight bore only superficial resemblance to anything that might pass for a boxing contest today. Fights were never decided on points and knockdowns were rare. Prize fights were wars of attrition in miniature. There were weight divisions of a fashion but these were not strictly adhered to: one fighter could easily find himself giving away a stone or more in weight to his opponent. Fighting ground was chosen with much deliberation according to its inaccessibility to the law and wherever was equidistant between both fighters' home towns. A quadrangle consisting of eight roped stakes, 24ft by 24, was erected. A line called the 'scratch mark' was carved into the turf between the two boxers. Rounds were of indeterminate length, ending only when a fighter was knocked to the ground. The stricken fighter would then have thirty seconds to drag himself to the scratch line or the fight was lost. Fights could last for hours with the tally of rounds sometimes etching into the hundreds. A fighter could not hit his opponent below the belt, head butt or gouge his eyes, but he was allowed to throw him to the ground and fall across him, or try to crush his ribs or break his back in a bear hug. The fight would be officiated by a referee and two umpires, each umpire representing one of the fighters. In an inversion of modern boxing etiquette, the referee would adjudicate from outside the ring whilst the seconds would be in the ring throughout the fight, falling to one knee at the end of a round to provide their man with a place to sit during the allotted thirty seconds' rest. Medical care was crude. A flagging fighter might be revived with a dose of brandy spat into his nostrils. At the end of these contests, fighters would invariably be caked in their own and their opponent's blood. They might not have been able to see much through swollen eyes. Broken fists and ribs

A statue of William 'Bendigo' Thompson, bare-knuckle champion of England.

were an occupational hazard. Deaths were not as common as people might imagine but were not alien to the game either.

On initial examination, prize fighting might appear a base pursuit practised by the common or the ignorant. Yet the sport could not have existed without the complicity of the upper classes and sympathetic quarters of the establishment. A good fighter needed stake-money in order to arrange a bout. The stake would be matched by his opponent and the winner would take all, minus expenses. The cash would invariably have been stumped up by a member of the nobility. He would make his money back and turn a profit in side bets if his man did well. Although prize fights were illegal they were covered in national periodicals with the seriousness and gravity of legitimate sporting events.[5] Railway companies ran private charters transporting crowds of supporters across the country to clandestine fight locations. Fights were often attended by nobility and the odd celebrity.[6]

Boxing had flourished in the Georgian age. Champions like the great Tom Cribb were celebrated as national heroes. The monarchy embraced the sport to the extent that, on his coronation, the Prince Regent requested a guard of honour comprised of veteran fighters. Thus, men who were technically criminals were publicly anointed by the royal family. The Victorian era demanded more circumspection from its respectable denizens and a palpable tension between the boxing fraternity and reputable society began to grow. Nature abhors a vacuum, so as the wealthy withdrew from the forefront of the fight game, the underworld advanced to occupy the vacant spaces. And the authorities, who up to this point had retained a high degree of ambivalence towards the whole affair, now sought to enforce the law with a vigour and violence previously unimagined. Nowhere were these differences more apparent than in Nottingham. And no East Midlander felt the full force of the change in social attitudes more than Harry Paulson.

Harry Paulson was a student of the great prize-fighter and champion of England William 'Bendigo' Thompson. Thanks in the main to boxers like Bendigo and his Hucknall-born

---

5. The loudest voice in print was Vincent Dowling, editor of the newspaper *Bells Life*, a paradoxical figure who was both an outspoken proponent of municipal police reform and prize fighting's senior apologist. Dowling was a semi-permanent presence at the ringside and an occasional referee.

6. Authors Charles Dickens and William Makepeace Thackeray were both enthusiastic supporters of prize fighting despite being outspoken opponents of public hanging.

arch-rival Ben Caunt, Nottingham was considered a town in serious contention with London as the capital of English prize fighting. Bendigo dominated the 1830s and '40s. Born in the slums of New Yard, now Trinity Square, Bendigo had shown an early aptitude for fighting and soon caught the attention of the boxing fraternity known as 'the Fancy'. He was small for a heavyweight but showed great mobility and ring generalship. He was a terrific showman and a flagrant but inspired cheat. A favoured technique would involve falling onto one knee when punched lightly giving the impression that he had been struck by a heavier blow. It was a disqualifiable offence but common practice amongst boxers who wanted to snatch an easy thirty seconds' rest. But Bendigo used it like a third fist to provoke and exasperate his adversaries into losing their tempers and committing more blatant disqualifiable fouls. Bendigo seemed to prefer winning this way but could fight like a savage when required to do so. An early contest saw Bendigo pick up an opponent and drive his head into the turf, temporarily blinding him.

Bendigo was extremely popular but considered for the most part a villain in the more respectable corners of the boxing fraternity. His unorthodox fighting style and predilection for questionable sportsmanship was bad enough, but it was his unapologetic ties to the more brutal elements of the sporting underworld that consistently sullied his reputation and obscured his genuine greatness as an athlete. Many boxers had retinues of thugs who accompanied them to fights and protected their interests at ringside. The Nottingham Lambs were the most feared and violent. Armed with lumps of wood they euphemistically called their 'old twigs', their presence at a fight often presaged a riot.

Bendigo was considered by many to be their leader. When Bendigo fought Ben Caunt in 1845, the contest was defined and the verdict arguably determined by the viciousness of the crowd. The referee was shamelessly intimidated and attempts were even made to strike Caunt during the match. Even Bendigo himself was accidentally clubbed in the confusion by one of his own supporters. The contest was seen as an absolute low point in the history of prize fighting. It also proved to be Bendigo's penultimate fight. He did not climb into the ring for another five years.

A lot was expected of Harry Paulson. He was a hard man whose toughness had been calcified by a life working as a ballast heaver and a navvy. Paulson was born in Newark but was a Nottingham man in spirit. He was a Lamb and a natural fighter. Harry Paulson was Bendigo's heir apparent.

Paulson's ring debut was quick and auspicious, easily dispatching his first opponent. For his second bout, an immediate step-up in class was desired and he was matched against the hot-tempered West Midlander Tom Paddock, Bendigo's final opponent.

In 1850, after an absence of five years, a forty-year-old Bendigo fought one last time in an inversion of the normal Bendigo performance. For once, Bendigo kept his illegal signature strategies under control. This time it was Paddock who sought to confound the champion with foul tactics and dirty blows, even managing to get away with kicking Bendigo in the chest with spiked boots. After a shaky start, Bendigo eventually exerted his dominance over Paddock with a succession of hard punches that induced a fit of vomiting in the younger man. The humiliation was too much. Paddock lost his temper and hit Bendigo with a foul blow so public he was forced to forfeit the contest.

In 1851 Bendigo groomed the reasonably inexperienced Paulson to face Tom Paddock. It would be the first of three clashes between the two boxers. At thirty-three years of age, Paulson was the older of the two fighters by five years. At twelve stone, both men were the same weight.

The fight took place in Sedgebrook, Lincolnshire. The battle lasted seventy-one rounds over ninety minutes, with Paulson eventually getting the better of Paddock. The police arrived to break up the fight but were driven from the field by the Lambs. Paddock joined the police in leaving the ring, to the noisy derision of the Lambs. In the confusion Paddock's seconds conceded defeat, throwing in the towel. It was an inadvertently compassionate decision as Paddock's eyes had been virtually punched shut by Paulson's heavy blows.

Police Superintendent William Wragg is dragged from his horse and beaten half to death by supporters at the Paulson/Paddock prize fight.

Three months later, on a sharp December afternoon, both men squared up to one other for the second time. The location was Cross End, Belper in Derbyshire. The first knockdown went to Paddock. First blood spilt caused a surge at ringside that breached the outer ring that was normally the province of the umpires and the referee. Unnoticed by the crowd, five horsemen appeared on the horizon and rode toward the fight.

The authorities had been perfectly aware that a large prize fight was going to occur in their jurisdiction. It was common practice for cat and mouse games to take place between the constabulary and the fight fraternity before a contest. Locations were often switched at the last minute and false destinations deliberately circulated by the Fancy to misdirect their enemies. If the police arrived at all it was normally too late, or in too few numbers, to do anything of real significance. On this occasion the location of the Paulson/Paddock match was revealed to the authorities. The problem was that the authorities in question consisted of a few magistrates and a police superintendent named William Wragg and little else. The distance was feared too great and time too much of a consideration to travel into Derby for reinforcements. So, the five men mounted up and rode into the volatile crowd, gambling on the fact that their rank and status would be enough to humble the assembly.

Jediah Strutt, one of the magistrates, called for the crowd to scatter. The normally fearless and explosive Paddock had a tendency to wilt in the face of authority. In his first bout with Paulson, Tom Paddock had fled the ring when the police arrived. He wavered now. His backers, without whose support Paddock could not fight, demanded that he carry on boxing or his purse would be withheld. Paddock acquiesced. Jediah Strutt and William Wragg steered their horses into the ring. Strutt began to read the Riot Act. The crowd went berserk. Nottingham Lambs and their Birmingham opposites, normally at each other's throats by this stage, united to attack the police officer. The superintendent was dragged from his horse and punched and kicked to the ground. The magistrates fled the field and rode to get the reinforcements they would have been wiser to arrive with in the first place. Wragg's unconscious body was picked up, thrown out of the ring and discarded.

In the light of the assault, a small army of police officers eager to comb the countryside and pick off retreating supporters was inevitable. The fight carried on. Paulson failed to make the scratch line – Paddock had won. The contest had lasted eighty rounds. Now that the fight had concluded the crowd were at liberty to scatter and make their way home as best they could. Paulson and Paddock left in a cart and coach respectively. Neither fighter got very far: both men were arrested.

Tom Paddock and Harry Paulson were tried at the county court in Derby. Paddock was characteristically contrite in the face of lawful authority. Paulson didn't appear to say much one way or the other. Both men were sentenced to ten months' hard labour. The sentence set a legal precedent for being the harshest ever handed down to any prize-fighter in the history of the sport, even including those few who had killed people in the ring.

Hard labour in Derby County Gaol consisted of a regimen of walking the tread-wheel, turning the two-handed crank and breaking stones. The labour was designed to be repetitive, exhausting, deliberately unproductive and painful. Daylight permitting, men were expected to work for ten to twelve hours a day. It was a routine designed to debilitate men from the labouring classes and would occasionally prove lethal to any member of the middle or upper classes unlucky enough to find themselves under the same sentence.[7] Paddock and Paulson served out their punishment with minimum fuss. The two fighters would not meet again for another three years.

Once Bendigo had retired, the boxing community degenerated into a flurry of claims and counter-claims as to who should be called the champion of England. A succession of elimination bouts open to every weight division tried to establish a definitive belt that, if successfully defended over a three-year period, would grant the holder the right to be called the undisputed champion. Everybody of note fought anybody of reputation in what would turn out to be domestic prize fighting's final blast of distinction. In this context, on St Valentine's Day 1854 in London's East End, Harry Paulson and Tom Paddock fought one another for the last time. As in their previous contest, Paulson could not make the scratch line and Paddock was permanently established as the greater of the two fighters.

Paddock was enjoying the finest period of his fighting career. As a fighter he had always been defined by a duo of contrary qualities: he was utterly fearless in the ring, and his temper invariably got the better of him. His spell in gaol seemed to have shaved the edge off of his bad humour. It afforded him greater discipline as a fighter and helped him to avoid the constant temptation to foul his opponents. It had been a bad habit that had kept the championship at perpetual arm's length. Paddock fought and beat every available contender of reputation. In 1856 Paddock eventually took the championship in a fifty-one-round contest against Harry Broome. But Paddock had little time to enjoy his victory – his health failed him and he would not fight again for two years.

Paulson was disillusioned. He had been heralded as the new Bendigo. To underscore the point, Bendigo had trained him, befriended him and been a conspicuous presence in his corner during fights. But the totemic company of the former champion had failed to rub off on him.

---

7. In 1895 Oscar Wilde was sentenced to a two-year stint of a slightly milder form of hard labour than that endured by Paddock and Paulson. The prison governor predicted that the regime would take its toll and Wilde would be dead two years after his release. Wilde's health was severely damaged during his spell at Reading Gaol. He died in 1900, one year beyond the governor's prediction.

Harry Paulson v. Tom Sayers. Paulson would suffer his most humiliating defeat at the hands of Sayers, despite being two-stone heavier and the 3-1 favourite.

Paulson had proved himself brave and gifted but just fell short of the qualities that might have made him truly great. He went back to being a navvy.

Harry Paulson stuck the hard, insular and frequently brutal world of the navigators for two years before being tempted back into the ring. On the surface, his return was inauspicious and shabby in comparison to the grandeur of 1851. He was fighting for £50 stakes. His opponent was Tom Sayers, a cocky middleweight who had apparently beaten everybody in his division yet had failed to unseat the champion Nat Langham. Sayers had claimed that the loss was due to poor health on his part and therefore inconsequential. He boasted that if he had been in good health he would have dispatched Langham like all the rest. Sayers did not bother to seek a rematch. As far as he was concerned, the middleweight division held little or no challenge for him anymore. He was glory-hungry and fancied his chances against bigger fighters. Sayers intended to take on the heavyweights if they would let him. His confidence was not shared by the Fancy, who refused to front him the necessary stake-money. Sayers was forced to find the cash himself.

Harry Paulson was two stones heavier than Tom Sayers. Paulson was the 3-1 favourite. His old rival Tom Paddock even placed a bet on him. On the surface it looked like easy money.

As soon as the fight began, Paulson's natural advantages proved to be dangerous liabilities. Sayers was unnaturally fast and mobile and he could punch. Paulson's frequent and unsuccessful attempts to lay his opponent low with powerful but comparatively clumsy blows expended his valuable energy reserves. Against all logic, Sayers drew first blood and set the precedent for the rest of the fight. He moved around Paulson, wearing him down and cutting him with precise and painful punches to the body and the head. Paulson's attempts to crush or throw Sayers proved as futile as his attempts to hit him and exacted further penalties against his stamina.

There was a savage irony at work. Paulson was supposed to be the new Bendigo. Bendigo had even overseen his training for the Sayers fight. But the man in front of Paulson was more Bendigo than Bendigo ever was. Paulson was outclassed. This was a brand new humiliation to add to all the others that had beset his life and career. But endurance and the will to persist, the quality that fighters called 'bottom', kept Paulson on his feet for 109 rounds. It took Sayers three hours and ten minutes to bleed Paulson sufficiently to the point where he could finally knock him unconscious. A knockout was rare among heavyweights but for a middleweight to knock out a man so much bigger and more experienced than himself heralded the arrival of a fighting prodigy. The knockout effectively ended Paulson's career as a boxer.

Sayers moved through the ranks of the heavyweights, beating them all. He met Paddock and cajoled and shamed the still stricken fighter into an ill-advised bout. This time it was the heavyweight who was counselled not to get into the ring with the smaller man. Paddock was punched to the point of blindness and then, in an honourable gesture, Sayers led his opponent back to his corner and quietly ended another career.

Sayers consolidated his legacy as the greatest of all domestic prize fighters by taking on the American giant John C. Heenan. Unofficially considered the first world championship prize fight, the clash between Heenan and Sayers ended in a draw when police stormed the ring. At the point when the fight was abandoned, the diminutive Sayers, having actually sustained a broken arm, had once again battered a bigger man to the point of virtual blindness.

Sayers verses Heenan marked the end of English bare-knuckle prize fighting. Sayers never fought again and the respective careers of his boxing contemporaries ended on notes of ignominy or else faded into obscurity. Bendigo was by this stage an ageing drunk and pub brawler. In 1860 Paddock took on another opponent when he was in poor health. Recovering from a knife wound sustained in an argument, Paddock fought Sam Hurst. Hurst was a giant and the physically stronger of the two men but a fighter of comparatively poor ability. Paddock was expected to win but was felled by a lucky but devastating punch that stove in three of his ribs and pierced his lung. Three years later, Paddock died of illness aged only thirty-nine.

Paulson began a slow decline into poverty and obscurity. He fought once more against Londoner Harry Tyson whom he beat in little over half an hour. The victory was inconsequential – Paulson's career was effectively at an end. Paulson maintained his friendship with Bendigo and bore witness to one of boxing's few happy endings. In the early 1870s, serving out a stint in gaol, Bendigo found Christianity. His character was radically transformed and Bendigo exchanged notoriety for a different kind of celebrity – he become an itinerant evangelist. He drew immense crowds to his revival meetings in the rougher parts of England's industrial cities. The conversion was genuine: his character was transformed and the respect and affection in which the old fighter was held eclipsed his earlier infamy.

In 1880 Bendigo hurt himself in a fall. In an echo of Tom Paddock's injury, Bendigo broke three ribs, one of them puncturing his lung. Complications arising from the injury proved fatal. Harry Paulson was present at Bendigo's side in the days before he died. Bendigo implored his old friend to convert. Paulson gently refused but kissed his mentor on the forehead. Bendigo died a few days later. Harry Paulson was a prominent figure amongst the thousands who watched Bendigo's coffin pass from his home in Beeston to his resting place in Nottingham.

At this point in time, America had taken prize fighting's mantle from the English and began to produce boxers that eclipsed the memory of our own. America had its transitional great in John L. Sullivan, the ferocious Irish American who initially fought bare fisted but became the sport's first gloved champion. The old world and the new converged when Sullivan and Paulson met in Nottingham toward the end of Paulson's life. Sullivan paid tribute to the old forgotten fighter, giving him £10.

Above left: Bendigo's monument in Bath Street.

Above right: Harry Paulson's memorial stone at Waverley Cemetery.

Paulson was never a great boxer in the sense that Paddock, Sayers and Bendigo were great. Of the bouts that we remember him for, Paulson won only one. He would invariably have regarded his own career as a failure. But his resilience, toughness and skill were an essential crucible in which the greatness of others was tried and defined. What was an outlaw profession that caused outsiders to view Nottingham with oscillating degrees of ambivalence is now a source of pride to the city. Nottingham can boast a legacy of outstanding fighters from Kirkland Laing to Carl Froch. It is a legacy that dates back to the foundations laid by men like Harry Paulson.

Nottingham monuments exist to Bendigo in the form of a sandstone memorial in Bath Street, a plaque commemorating his birth in Trinity Square, and a statue above The Hermitage pub in Sneinton. There is a town named after him in Australia and he even merits a passing mention in Herman Melville's novel, *Moby Dick*.[8] Paulson's memorial stone can found somewhere in Waverley Cemetery. It is in a better state of preservation than his mentor's because it has had fewer visitors to erode its lettering. Inscribed on the tombstone is the epitaph:

Harry Paulson
Died Dec 11th 1890
In his 72nd year
The memorial stone was erected by his friends and admirers in appreciation of his upright and manly conduct in the ring.

---

8. In chapter thirty-seven of Moby Dick, Captain Ahab says, 'I laugh and hoot at ye, ye cricket players, ye pugilists, ye deaf Burkes and blinded Bendigoes!' John 'Deaf' Burke was the fighter Bendigo defeated in 1839 to become champion of England for the first time.

8

Life and Death of a County Gaol

'It will be seen by the foregoing report that this prison is at present in a bad state, and that the great majority of the inmates must necessarily leave it worse than they entered.'
Report by Inspector of Prisons on Nottingham County Gaol, 1850.

In 1316 Nottingham was subject to the worst famine in its entire history. Food supplies were quickly exhausted. Horses were eaten, followed by domestic animals and then vermin. Before long, cannibalism became an ugly presence in the medieval town. Children were stolen and killed for food. Nothing was taboo. Many prisoners placed in the town's gaol were overpowered by their cell mates, murdered and eaten.

There is nothing in Nottingham's penal history that comes close to matching the horror of what happened during the 1316 famine. But even during the most placid periods of pre-twentieth-century convict life, being a prisoner in Nottingham was a deeply unpleasant experience. By the close of the nineteenth century, the two principle locations a criminal could be locked up for any length of time were the House of Correction[9] and the County Gaol. The County Gaol was, on many levels, the worst of the two sites and the first to be closed when prison policy became firmly dictated by the Home Office.

Gaols as we begin to understand them only came into being in the eighteenth century. Nottingham County Gaol was constructed during this period but there had been gaol cells and court rooms of one form or another on the site since the Middle Ages. The first gaol of any significance in Nottingham was established by King John in 1202. Medieval gaols were privately owned by the rich and powerful and anybody incarcerated there was completely at the mercy of these men. There was nothing by way of law to stop prisoners being detained for indefinite periods of time in squalid conditions. Attempts to regulate the system were introduced by

---

9. Houses of Correction were introduced in the sixteenth century, originally designed as places of work for those on the fringes of criminal society. Tramps, beggars, the lazy, the unemployed and prostitutes were all sent to these institutions. In time they also became places where petty criminals would serve out short sentences lasting a couple of months and prisoners would be held on remand before trial. Towards the end of the nineteenth century, Houses of Correction were also execution sites and became places where serious criminals would serve out lengthy prison sentences.

Right: Cannibalism in Nottingham's medieval gaols.

Below: Nottingham County Gaol.

Henry IV who decreed that Justices of the Peace were the only people who could put a man or a woman in gaol. The gaol in question was the Common Gaol (where an individual could even live quite comfortably if they had enough money), but generally speaking incarceration was rare. Punishment tended to be immediate and punitive.

Nottingham County Gaol was an impressive structure, incorporating and located directly beneath the county courts of the Shire Hall on High Pavement. The gaol was cut into the sandstone cliff face that overlooked the stretch of land that would eventually become the slum of Narrow Marsh. Like any gaol of the period, it was essentially a holding place for people awaiting trial, or else a place where minor sentences were served and debtors worked off their deficit. Lengthy prison sentences were not the norm at this point in history. If a man or woman were convicted of a serious offence then they would either be executed or else transported overseas to the various prison colonies in Great Britain's burgeoning empire. Gaols were filthy and brutal places with very little centralised regulation, gaol being the sole responsibility of the local justices.

There was little or no subsidy for gaols and the institutions were largely expected to fund themselves. Guards were not properly trained and many were paid poorly or not at all. Guards were, however, permitted to levy charges on the convict population by way of commission for providing better cells, extra food, bedding, fuel and alcohol. If prisoners incurred debts to the gaoler then they were expected to stay in gaol until they had found the money to pay him back, irrespective of their release date. If a prisoner were on remand and subsequently found not guilty, but owed the gaoler money, then the gaoler was within his rights to detain the prisoner until he or she had paid back what they owed.

Prisoners were not properly categorised or separated; men, women and children were often thrown together. Petty criminals were obliged to mix with hardened criminals and the untried with the convicted. The ingredients for every manner of corruption and abuse were present.

Although most accepted the status quo, there were a vocal minority of people in positions of influence and authority who strongly objected to the state of affairs. Most notable among them was John Howard, the celebrated (but generally ignored in his lifetime) prison reformer. Howard travelled the length and breadth of the country visiting the nation's gaols and chronicling what he found there. John Howard came to Nottingham County Gaol in the 1770s. His observations provide a window into East Midlands prison life in the late eighteenth century. In his writings Howard left a record of the gaoler's name, salary, the fees he was permitted to charge, as well as the allowances afforded the county's prisoners:

GAOLER, Richard Bonigton
Salary, £20
Fees, Debtors 14s 8d
Felons, 14s
Transports, £7 7s 6d each
Licence, Beer
PRISONERS
Allowances, Debtors, three half-pennyworth of bread a day
Felons, three half-pennyworth of bread and a half-penny of money every day (weight of three-penny loaf in Jan 177, 1lb 141/2oz in September 1779, 2lb 3oz.

Howard also observed that the female prisoners shared a bed, and although prisoners could bathe in a 'large and commodious bath,' the bath water was essentially river water. He called the gaol an 'unwholesome dungeon' but, by the standards of the time, it was fairly average. All of the above concurred with John Howard's condemnation of the prison system at large.

Although Howard was seen as an eccentric oddity in his lifetime, he did succeed in changing the law, making it technically illegal, amongst other things, for men and women to be incarcerated together. But the law was impossible to enforce as there was very little centralised control of the prison system. Local governments were free to ignore the law, without repercussion. Howard did however manage to plant the seeds for a second wave of reform that would take hold in the following century. The long, slow process of dragging gaols out of the past had begun.

In the 1830s, under Robert Peel's Gaol Act, every gaol or prison became subject to annual inspections. Nottingham County Gaol would receive regular visits from the Inspector of Prisons. The reports would be relentlessly critical of the institution. Initially this did not matter, as there was no legal precedent to enforce any recommendation made – power to implement changes still rested with the local justices. A cycle of reproof and denial began. On an annual basis, the inspector would berate the gaol for the numerous ways in which it fell short of the national standard, whilst the justices remained resolute in their inability (or disinclination) to implement the inspector's recommendations. But as the century progressed and the reform lobby became more and more powerful, the County Gaol was to become ever more of an anachronism and embarrassment.

The prison inspector's reports provide the best insight into the heart of Nottingham County Gaol. They make for disturbing and occasionally comical reading and shed the most illuminating light on what a Nottinghamshire convict had to endure on a daily basis. The reports also graphically illustrate why the County Gaol was considered by many to be amongst the nation's worst prisons.

It wasn't that the County Gaol's regime was a particularly brutal one. The main punishments employed would have been isolation in the dark cells, food stoppages, hard labour, flogging and birching (punishments that, in truth, were very rarely employed). It was an average regimen by the standards of the time and there is more evidence of violence being meted out against the gaol's employees than the other way round. The prison's appalling reputation rested in the fact that it was about as badly run, designed and organised as it was possible to be. Everything about the place facilitated disease, escape and criminal levels of incompetence.

The first thing a prisoner would notice on entering the gaol was the stench of bodily waste. Throughout the decades, inspectors complained of the terrible smells emanating from, in and around the gaol. In the 1830s, the state of a particular prison toilet was so rancid that it was in danger of putting a halt to Sunday chapel. In the 1840s, the prison doctor abjectly refused to use the infirmary because it was too near to a foul-smelling privy. In the 1860s, the smells wafting over the gaol walls from Narrow Marsh's numerous ash toilets elicited strong complaints from the gaol staff. Perhaps the worst odour ever to assail the nostrils of a Nottingham convict was that of a corpse that had been left to rot in the infirmary due to the absence of a proper storage space for the dead.

Medical disruption was par for the course in the County Gaol, but surgeons were generally amongst the more competent of the institution's employees. The surgeon would visit the sick on a daily basis and made sure he visited every prisoner twice a week. Nottingham County Gaol surgeons were generally very dedicated and worked to make the prisoners' lives better. It was an uphill struggle nevertheless, with the general health of the convict population undermined by poor diet, bad administration (the infirmary often being occupied by debtors) and damp, appalling conditions. Ailments the surgeon might find himself treating were the itch, diarrhoea, low fever and dysentery as well as the steady stream of lunatic convicts awaiting transfer to Broadmoor or the County Asylum. The surgeon also had the power to discipline those who feigned illness ('shammers') with a spell in solitary confinement. The average health of prisoners was one of the few things to gradually improve as the century progressed, thanks to the dedication and technical innovations of many of the medical staff. In the 1850s, a Dr Arnott devised a machine worked by prisoners that would blast hot air into the least ventilated parts of the prison, improving conditions for many convicts. Such levels of competence and innovation were sadly the exception rather than the norm. By dint of comparison, the religious life of Nottingham County Gaol was positively shambolic.

The year 1840 marked the first concrete mention of the chaplain in the prison reports when a prison chaplain heard a condemned man's confession in one of the cells overlooking Narrow Marsh. Unfortunately the confession was audible to the residents in the slum beneath the prison walls and the convict was forced to suffer the humiliation of hearing his intimate confidence being repeated back to him, 'bawled about in the streets below.'

The chaplain was at the centre of a minor controversy two years later. A feud had erupted between the clergyman and a sizable contingent of the convict population over his refusal to contribute to a Christmas fund for the prisoners. Adamant that his charity should not extend to the financial support of 'inordinate eating and drinking', even at Christmas, the chaplain refused to put his hand in his pocket. Three influential convicts retaliated by organising a church boycott. That same year the chaplain was once again on the back foot, explaining to the Inspector of Prisons how it came to be that a mysterious woman had preached in his pulpit. The chaplain's response was hardly to his credit – he'd had no idea that any such incident had taken place.

As a rule, the levels of moral instruction in Nottingham County Gaol were generally frowned upon by the prison inspectors, and the fact that the chaplain from time to time allowed a common gaoler (often regarded as little better than criminals themselves) to teach religious instruction was held in utter contempt. A change of chaplain twenty years later brought a little more order to the prison's religious affairs. He seemed a man in step with the times, advocating a half-way house for the freshly released, as well as the separation of prisoners from one another during their incarceration.

Separation was consistent with the pervading wisdom of the age. The eighteenth-century methodology of idly lumping all of the prisoners together irrespective of classification was anathema to the Victorian penal reformer. The compassion of the early reformers was slowly being supplanted by a cruel-to-be-kind approach to prison administration. The perceived wisdom of the time was that prisoners who talked to one another were more than likely to be about the business of mutual corruption than communal edification, so it was considered best to separate them and impose a complete ban on talking. It was also believed that prisoners who spent the day in idle repose would be better engaged in acts of tedious or painful hard labour. Whether the labour produced anything practical or not was largely immaterial. Idleness was a source of constant complaint in the prison reports and warranted mention in 1838, 1842, 1844, 1845, 1850 (where it was seen as a contributing factor to prison illness) and in 1851 (where it was mentioned on three separate occasions). The following year hard labour was implemented in earnest and prisoners were obliged to break stones, walk a tread-wheel and operate a crank. To begin with, the crank was probably just a rudimentary water pump that prisoners were required to work all day. By the 1870s, standards had slackened a little. Nobody appeared to be walking the treadmill or breaking stones anymore, but the County Gaol had managed to buy a refined version of the crank. The modified crank was essentially a box full of sand with a handle attached to an internal mechanism that resisted the push and pull of any prisoner forced to turn it. Prisoners assigned to the crank were obliged to turn it 10,000 times a day. General prison labour consisted of cobbling, sewing, knitting, woodwork, oakum picking and the laundry. The women worked the laundry.

In reality, there were never very many women in the County Gaol. In the 1838 report, there were on average only three female convicts present at any one time. In the 1850 report,

Top: An exercise yard inside Nottingham County Gaol. The yard also doubled as a place of execution.

Above left: A standard three-man cell in the County Gaol.

Above right: The Dark Cells were used for punishment and possibly to detain men condemned to death.

the gaol held thirty-four men and seven women at the time of the inspector's visit. Despite the low numbers, accommodating women was an ongoing problem. The few women resident were shunted around the gaol over the decades. In the 1830s the only bath in the gaol was in the women's wing. Whenever a male prisoner was bathed the women had to be removed from sight and locked up. Later on, the female population were moved from damp cells near the debtors' wing to cells overlooking the slums of Narrow Marsh. They were subsequently moved from the cells overlooking the Marsh to cells beneath the governor's residence for fear that they would communicate with the inhabitants of the criminal slum below. They lived underneath the governor's residence until those cells were condemned for being too damp. The women eventually ended up being housed in the vagrants' ward.

The design of the gaol was abysmal. The entire building had a reputation for structural unsoundness. In 1724, the court had fallen through the floor into the cells below, ripping the flesh from one man's leg and exposing the bone as well as incurring the wrath of the judge (who was hearing a case at the time). The judge threatened to fine Nottingham for £2,000 in damages as a consequence.

New wings were periodically added to the existing structure without any real thought being given to practicality or security. Private houses overlooked some of the exercise yards and the lock to the main gate of the gaol was on the outside of the prison. The architecture, location and administration of Nottingham County Gaol seemed to encourage escapes and escape attempts were numerous. In the 1838 report, the most pressing problems amongst the convict population were said to be frequent attempts to break out of the County Gaol. In 1837 a female convict freed herself from her room and lowered herself into the yard on an improvised rope made from bedding. She was caught trying to scale the wall and climb down to Narrow Marsh. She was re-apprehended and placed in solitary with reduced rations. Two years later, a male prisoner climbed onto the wall via the roof of an outside toilet. He was unlucky enough to be sharing a cell with an informer who had been 'detained to give evidence against the Chartists.' The informer immediately raised the alarm. The escapee got clear of the prison and took refuge yards away in his father's house on Garners Hill. He was found hiding up a chimney.[10]

Not all escapes were quite so amusing. In the 1840s, six prisoners bound for the colonies beat a guard half to death trying to get out of the gaol. In another escape attempt, a guard was hit about the head with a scrubbing brush by two prisoners who had, completely unobserved, climbed an interior wall and joined a cleaning party near the entrance to the gaol. The prisoners took the guard's key and managed to get as far as the front entrance before being tackled by another guard. The governor himself was present and immediately came to the guard's assistance, tussling with the convicts and helping to secure their recapture. In the 1870s, four more prisoners escaped through the roof of the infirmary, three of them successfully evading capture.

In the 1840 report, the Inspector of Prisons stated that, 'no officer, however alert, can properly discharge his duty or effective superintendence over the prisoners with such obstructions as are placed in his way by the construction of the prison.' This presupposed that Nottingham County Gaol's officers were alert in the first place. Early prison reports expressed concern over a guard who would take the keys of the prison into town with him. This was not an isolated incident. Cavalier thoughtlessness among the prison staff would undermine the gaol's effectiveness throughout its lifespan. In the 1830s, a guard admitted that he might have accidentally permitted visiting prostitutes to enter the prison grounds. In the mid-1860s, another guard excelled himself in dereliction of duty and contributed to one of the County Gaol's more humiliating episodes.

---

10. The informer would later complain of being tormented by the ghost of the recently-executed murderer John Driver.

Nottingham House of Correction, another victim of Edmund Du Cane's reforms. (Picture courtesy of Nottingham City Council and www.picturethepast.org.uk)

Prisoners were often left unsupervised by the guards. This was bad enough in itself, but on one occasion a prisoner with a history of feigning illness and insanity was left on his own in the exercise yard with a ladder propped against the yard wall. The prisoner scaled the wall and made his escape. He was captured two hours later but the damage had been done to the gaol's already suspect reputation for security. The Inspector of Prisons was naturally incensed at the guard's incompetence, so much so that he could not fully bring himself to blame the escaped prisoner for failing to resist the temptation placed in his way by prison staff. Five years later, two guards went one better and deliberately aided a debtor in his escape. Their resignation was demanded as a consequence.

In 1877 the Inspector of Prisons paid his last visit to Nottingham County Gaol. The law was changing. Home Secretary Edmund Du Cane had finally managed to bring prisons under the direct control of the Home Office. New prisons were being built around the country that fully embraced the doctrines of discipline, regimentation, hard labour, security and silence (the Separate System having been abandoned due to complete isolation inducing insanity in many of the prisoners forced to endure it). Under Du Cane's administration, any prison that did not fall in line with government standards would close. To be fair to Nottingham County Gaol, there had been a slow crawl toward reform. A change of governor in the middle years of the century seemed to have had a marginally positive effect on administration, but it was too little too late.

On 1 December 1876, fire gutted the court rooms above the prison. The prison itself was undamaged – this would prove to be a stroke of irony. On 1 April 1878, the Home Office officially ordered the County Gaol permanently shut, though the gutted court rooms were rebuilt and continue to be used well into the twentieth century. The County Gaol was closed the same year that electric lighting made its first appearance on the streets of Nottingham. The old had gone; the new was on its way. Before long, construction began on Bagthorpe Gaol. The brand-new, government-approved prison replaced all other existing Nottingham gaols. The site is now the current location for HM Nottingham Prison. The county courts at the Shire Hall were eventually closed in 1986. Eleven years later the entire site was converted into the Galleries of Justice, a crime and punishment museum permanently bearing witness to Nottingham's penal incompetence.

The list of intake in 1861 at Nottingham County Gaol:

Murder	4
Attempted murder	3
Abortion, attempt to procure birth	2
Concealment of birth	8
Bestiality	2
Rape	4
Indecent assaults	4
Unlawful wounding	10
Forgery	4
Arson	1
Perjury	1
Bigamy	1
Horse stealing	1
Cattle stealing	1
Burglary	9
Housebreaking	6
Highway robbery	1
Larceny:	
simple	59
from the person	4
servants	1
under Criminal Justice Act	48
under Juvenile Offenders Act	13
Embezzlement	2
Receiving stolen property	1
Obtaining by false pretences	6
Armed night poaching	5
Game trespass	1
Uttering counterfeit coin	3
Garden robbing	11
Assaults	24
Want of sureties	44
Other summary convictions	17
Attempting to commit suicide	1
Deserters	10

Ingredients of Nottingham County Gaol prisoners' diet in the late nineteenth century:

Soup
In every pint:
The meat and liquor from 6 ounces of the neck, legs and shins of beef, weighed with the bone, previous to cooking.
1 ounce of onions or leeks.
1 once of Scotch barley.
2 ounces of carrots, parsnips, turnips or another cheap vegetable with pepper and salt.
On Tuesdays and Saturdays the meat liquor of the previous day is to be added.

Suet Pudding
1½ ounces of suet.
6 ½ ounces of flour, and about 8 ounces of water to make 1 pound.

Indian-Meal Pudding
To consist of ½ pint of skimmed milk, to every 6 ounces of skimmed meal.

Ingredients of gruel
To every pint, 2 ounces of coarse Scotch oatmeal with salt.

9

Mr and Mrs Thompson: How a Nottingham Girl Dethroned the King of Cat Burglars

In his short story, *The Illustrious Client*, Arthur Conan Doyle put these words into the mouth of his great fictional detective Sherlock Holmes:

'A complex mind,' said Holmes. 'All great criminals have that. My old friend Charlie Peace was a violin virtuoso.'

Around about the same time a play entitled, *The Life and Times of Charles Peace*, was performed, causing great controversy at the Grand Theatre, Gravesend. The climax of the play involved a staged execution in which a real hangman simulated the execution of master criminal Charles Peace on a genuine gallows. The theatrical display was deemed so tasteless it raised questions in Parliament.

With the exception of Jack the Ripper, no single Victorian criminal provoked more interest and was surrounded by more mythology than Charles Frederick Peace. He was a burglar with seemingly supernatural powers of entry, a double murderer, a master of disguise and one of history's most eccentric criminal personalities. He began his career in the North of England and ended it in the South. He spent time in Nottingham and his association the city contributed significantly to his eventual undoing.

Charles Peace was born in May 1832 in Sheffield. His father was a cobbler who had, in his time, worked in the mines and claimed to have joined the circus. So, when Peace was born, his father could boast, telling stories of his colourful career as a trainer of wild beasts. Charles Peace would inherit his father's dissatisfaction with the status quo.

Peace dabbled with legitimate employment for a spell but was crippled in the steel mills when a chunk of hot metal entered his leg – he would walk with a limp for the rest of his life. For a young man predisposed to an irregular path, two options seemed to present themselves to him: he had begun to dabble in petty crime, but also showed great aptitude as an entertainer. He was regarded as a gifted actor and displayed an even greater talent for music. His mastery of the violin earned him the title, 'Modern Paganini'. Peace chose crime, although in the course of time he would use his arsenal of theatrical tricks to further his criminal career and avoid capture by the police. But for the time being he was simply learning the ropes and little distinguished him from the host of thieves who plagued any industrial city of the era.

A portrait of Charles Peace, Victorian England's most wanted man.

Charles Peace's criminal apprenticeship was long and brutal but effective. For Peace, the 1850s and '60s were largely defined by time spent in gaol. In 1851 Peace served one month for possession of stolen goods. In 1854 he was convicted of burglary and sentenced to four years' imprisonment. He was released in 1858. In 1859 Charles Peace married. His chosen bride was a widow named Hannah Ward who had a son from a previous marriage. The pacifying allure of domesticity and parenthood failed to work its magic on Charles Peace. Within a year he was back in prison again. This time, Peace was caught unearthing a bag of stolen goods that he had buried after a burglary. Peace resisted arrest with vicious gusto. It was his first recorded instance of violence and would become a signature response to any situation that left him feeling cornered.

Peace was sentenced to six years. He was set free early in 1864, and may have even been released for good behaviour. If this is true, it may also have inspired him to try his hand at legitimate business. Peace set up shop as a picture framer and by all accounts was very good at his job. His family went to church. All the outward signs of respectability were present. Whether his attempts at family life were genuine but the pull of crime was too much to resist or whether it was always a smoke screen for his criminal activities, Charles Peace was arrested for burglary in 1864. He was to receive the most severe sentence so far and was locked away for eight years.

Whatever had inclined Peace to good behaviour in the past was distinctly absent as he served out his sentence at Wakefield House of Correction, and he tried to escape. At least for the first part of his sentence, Charles Peace must have conformed to the prison rules as he was given the job of assisting with prison repairs, a privilege normally only assigned to the compliant. Taking full advantage of the trust placed in him, Peace managed to smuggle a small ladder and a saw into his cell. He cut a hole in the ceiling and tried to pull himself up onto the prison roof. A guard walked in on him. Peace knocked the guard out. What had been planned as a stealthy exit had now become by necessity a manic sprint for freedom. Peace ran along an unstable prison roof. He lost his footing and fell into the grounds of the governor's house – he was eventually caught hiding in the governor's bedroom.

For the remainder of his sentence, Charles Peace was bounced around the prison system. He spent time locked in the pitch-black punishment cells. He may have attempted suicide. He probably took part in an uprising at Chatham Prison for which he would have been flogged. When Charles Peace was released in 1872 he was a middle-aged man who had spent over a decade of his life in gaol.

In 1875 Peace and his family moved from Sheffield to the respectable suburb of Darnall. Next door but one to Peace was the residence of Arthur and Katherine Dyson. A friendship soon developed between the new neighbours.

Charles Peace murders PC Nicholas Cock.

The exact nature of the relationship between Charles Peace and Katherine Dyson is not crystal clear. Peace claimed that she was his mistress. Dyson always denied it. Their friendship was undeniably intense and seemingly replete with circumstantial evidence to neither person's credit. They were seen together at pubs and music halls. They argued. They met together in a deserted house that separated their own properties. They exchanged secret correspondence. But after an intense three months, the friendship, on Katherine's insistence, ended. At this point, Peace had become an omnipresent and obsessive threat to the Dysons' marital stability. Arthur Dyson forced the issue and delivered a card formally demanding that Peace keep away. Peace exploded. He confronted the Dysons, produced a pistol and threatened them with violence. The Dysons went to the police and a warrant was issued for the arrest of Charles Peace on the charge of threatening behaviour. Peace and his family packed up and moved to Hull before the warrant was served. But Charles Peace was not done with the Dysons. The Dysons had moved house but it didn't take a great deal of effort for Peace to find out where they had gone. He tracked them down and made his presence and hostile intentions known to them all over again. However, the Dysons were given a short reprieve as Peace was forced to defer his vendetta in the light of something far more troubling.

As was his custom, Peace set up a legitimate business front in his new neighbourhood and carried out burglaries at night time. At Whalley Range in Manchester, Charles Peace was leaving a freshly burgled house, when Police Constable Nicholas Cock appeared, seemingly out of nowhere and attempted to arrest him. Peace pulled a gun and fired twice at the approaching officer. The first bullet was probably a warning shot. The second bullet hit the constable in the chest, fatally wounding him. It took the constable forty minutes to die.

A couple of pieces of luck saved Peace from arrest: the constable never gave a proper description of his assailant, and two brothers (William and John Habron) were arrested for his murder. The arrests were highly dubious. Both brothers had had a stormy relationship with the police and had previously threatened local officers with death. But beyond that, there was little actual evidence to convict them. Nevertheless, they were arrested and put on trial for murder.

The cat burglar's luck held out throughout their trial. John Habron was acquitted. His brother William was found guilty and sentenced to death. Due to William's age (he was eighteen years old) and a request for mercy from the jury, the sentence was commuted to life imprisonment. Throughout the trial, the real killer was an anonymous presence in the public gallery.

Now in the clear, Charles Peace turned his attention back to the Dysons. One evening in November, Peace was loitering around the back of the Dysons' house in Banner Cross. He waited until Katherine had left the house to go to the toilet in the outside privy. Peace appeared. Katherine screamed. Her husband stormed into the garden. Peace ran away. Arthur followed him.

Arthur was a large man, a foot taller than Charles Peace. He was also a railway engineer. Peace was short but (despite his limp) agile as a monkey and strong. Moreover, any size difference was moot as Peace had brought his gun with him. He fired two shots at Arthur Dyson. The first missed – but the second hit Dyson in the head and killed him. Peace had committed his second murder in public. With a documented history of threats and intimidation against the Dysons and a fresh killing under his belt, the North was no longer a safe place for Charles Peace. Peace and his family packed up and fled. They headed south and eventually took up residence in Nottingham.

The murder of Arthur Dyson marked Charles Peace's graduation to criminal celebrity. A reward of £100 was posted for his capture. A description was circulated by the police emphasising his strange appearance. Charles Peace's physiognomy was a gift to the sensationalists and Penny Dreadful novelists of the period. His face was distinctly simian. He had the ability to mould his features as if they were made of rubber, distorting his face to assume a visage radically different from his own. He looked significantly older than he was, the police inadvertently adding ten years to his age in their wanted posters. In addition to his limp he had at least one finger missing from his left hand. How Peace had come to lose the finger became grist to the mill for criminal-myth makers up and down the county. Some claimed that he had deliberately blasted a finger or two off to tamper with the official police descriptions of him. Some thought that the fingers had been chopped off by a butcher in a botched robbery. More measured imaginations believed that the accident had happened while Peace was cleaning his guns. In all probability the injury, like his limp, had been sustained during his time working in industry.

The fact that Peace had committed murder with a gun made him automatically exotic in the eyes of the public. Victorian murder was generally utilitarian in nature. Knives, chisels, bludgeons and the ubiquitous cut-throat razor were the weapons of choice in the heat of the moment. Sophisticates used poison. Guns were rare. They were, however, stock-in-trade for professional burglars. This was not necessarily because burglars were more prone to committing murder than other criminals; it was a practical measure, as affluent houses were more likely to have armed servants guarding the wealth of their employers. It was simply a practical matter of self-defence.

By the time Peace arrived in Nottingham, he was the country's most wanted man and already on his way to becoming a full-blown figure of romantic myth. Peace was believed to have taken residence in Drury Hill, the street that ran through the centre of the rough Broad Marsh area of Nottingham. He is said to have hidden out in Trinity Square. It is also suspected that he stayed for a while at the notorious Brewhouse Yard. Situated at the base of the castle, Brewhouse Yard was a haven for criminals owing to an administrative error dating back to Norman times that placed the area outside the legally-recognised administrative boundaries of the town. The residents didn't pay rates. They seldom received any help from local government but were not overly troubled by the law either.

Many exploits are attributed to Peace's time in Nottingham. Police are supposed to have searched a barber's shop for him, not realising that the customer sat in front of them (whose face was obscured by foam) was their man. He is also supposed to have stolen a piano from under the noses of the staff at The Tavern pub. The most often told Nottingham story is probably true. In bed with a local woman at the time, the house where Peace was staying was raided by the police. The detectives came upon Peace, not properly realising who he was. The fugitive requested that the police, for modesty's sake, allowed him to get dressed in private. The police left the room and went down stairs. Peace disappeared out the window.

While this may not be the most compelling anecdote in the Peace canon, it is significant as the woman who shared Peace's bed was almost certainly Susan Grey. Like Hannah Ward before her, Susan Grey was a widow. She was reasonably well educated but given to drinking and taking snuff. Grey was sharing the same lodging house as Charles Peace but living with a man at the time. Grey soon fell under Peace's influence. She passed over the man she was living with in favour of Peace, becoming his lover and accomplice.

Nottingham was too dangerous a place for Charles Peace to remain there for long. Soon it was time to leave. He took his wife, stepson and new mistress to London. Peace and his mini-harem settled in Peckham. In London, Charles Peace established his most successful and respectable front, while in secret perpetuating his most subversive repudiation of Victorian morality. Peace re-established his picture-framing business and became known as a local eccentric, beloved within the community. He attended church, performed musical recitals and indulged in endearingly quirky hobbies such as inventing, creating, amongst other things, an anti-smoke helmet for firemen. During the evening, he would rob the surrounding areas blind (being very careful not to commit any crime in Peckham where he lived). The same instrument case in which he carried his violin to musical evenings would double as a tool box for his burglary equipment. Peace's living arrangements were equally scandalous. Susan Grey passed herself off as Charles Peace's wife, both answering to the names Mr and Mrs Thompson. Peace and Grey had a child together. Charles Peace's real wife lived in the basement with her son and passed herself off as the housekeeper.

Left: Drury Hill, a suspected hiding place of Charles Peace. (Picture courtesy of Nottingham City Council and www.picturethepast.org.uk)

Opposite above: Brewhouse Yard, a favourite place of sanctuary for the criminal classes. Charles Peace was believed to have stayed here when he was on the run for murder.

Opposite below: Drury Hill as it is today, a nondescript alley sandwiched between two cafés.

BREWHOUSE YARD
The Museum of Nottingham Life
WELCOME

Broad Marsh Bus & Coach Station
Nottingham Castle
Nottingham Railway Station

Low Pavement
Lace Market — Castle

jass
cafe

In October 1878, Charles Peace burgled a house in Blackheath. He was negligent in concealing a light, which was spotted from the street by Edward Robinson, a local police constable. Reinforcements gathered and a small group of police officers moved in on the burglar. Two of them went to the front door. They pressed the bell, their intention being to flush the burglar out of the rear of the building. Peace climbed out of the back window but was confronted by Robinson. Peace bolted and Robinson gave chase. Peace had been in this situation before and responded in exactly the same fashion: he opened fire. Peace would later claim that he intended the shots as warnings. He fired five times at the advancing policeman. The final shot hit Robinson in the arm at point-blank range. It would have pierced the policeman's chest had his arm not been raised at the time. With one good arm left, Edward Robinson tackled Peace and hung on until his colleagues arrived. Peace was subdued and then arrested.

Charles Peace was charged with the attempted murder of a police officer. He was in as much trouble as he had ever been in, but the situation could have been worse. Peace gave his name as John Ward. The police had no idea who was actually in their custody and Peace was able to successfully maintain the façade right the way through his trial. He was found guilty and sentenced to life imprisonment at Pentonville Prison.

Susan Grey is generally held as responsible for blowing Peace's cover. Grey and Hannah Ward packed up and left the area as soon as Peace was arrested. Grey's betrayal had a number of possible motives: she had always been something of a liability, with the chance that her heavy drinking might lead to indiscretions. But Grey was also pragmatic. Peace was in prison; he wasn't ever coming out unless he escaped, which this time was highly unlikely. She needed or wanted money and there was still a £100 reward up for anyone offering information leading to the whereabouts of Charles Peace. The police were informed and Peace's identity was exposed. Charles Peace would now stand trial for the murder of Arthur Dyson and if found guilty would, in all likelihood, hang.

Under guard, Peace was taken to Sheffield for a hearing. Throughout the train journey Peace's behaviour was erratic to say the least. He was obsessed with relieving himself and wanted to make a toilet stop at virtually every station. Going to the toilet on the train was impractical as there were no aisles linking the carriages and subsequently no toilet on board. To compensate, the guards had been issued with paper bags for the prisoner to defecate in. If he wanted to urinate he could go out of the window. The guards were prepared for the eventuality but not for the volume of requests from Peace to go to the toilet. As they approached Sheffield, Peace decided that he needed to go to relive himself once again. The guards opened the window and averted their eyes. Peace had taken advantage of the law's modesty once before in Nottingham; he tried to the same trick again and threw himself out of the window of the moving train. One of the guards caught him by the foot. Peace struggled to dislodge himself and eventually hit the track. The train was travelling somewhere in the vicinity of forty miles per hour.

Whether Peace had intended to escape or kill himself is unclear. He should have been killed but the combination of snow on the track and the guard halting his momentum saved his life. Nevertheless he knocked himself senseless and sustained a nasty wound to his scalp.

In early 1879 Charles Peace stood trial for murder. Katherine Dyson had moved to America after her husband's death. She was recalled as a witness. Despite the defence's ruthless attempts to undermine her credibility by insisting that she had been romantically involved with the accused, Dyson held her ground. There were enough witnesses besides Katherine who could place Peace in the area around the time of the shooting, and had heard him barking threats of murder at the Dysons, to make a guilty verdict a matter of formality. The jury made their decision in less than fifteen minutes: Charles Peace was sentenced to hang.

As Peace prepared for death, a change came over him. The guilty verdict seemed to have sucked all of the usual defiance out of him. He talked to a clergyman and confessed to the

Charles Peace attempts a desperate escape from a moving train.

murder of the police officer in Manchester. At first his confession was met with cynicism, but after he corroborated details that only the police could have known and offered a ballistics match between the bullets in his own gun and the slug which had been dug out of the body of the murdered policeman, his story was taken seriously. William Habron was released and handsomely compensated for the two years he had spent locked away for a murder he had nothing to do with.

It is easy to be cynical about deathbed conversions, but Charles Frederick Peace seems to have reconciled himself with God in his final days. He had freed an innocent man. He did not deny his crimes. He met death with a degree of resignation that was distinctly out of character. Hangman William Marwood expected a struggle but, despite a last flutter of belligerence over breakfast, Charles Peace was meek on his final day. As the hood was about to be placed over his head, he requested that the executioner wait until he had heard the chaplain finish his Bible reading. Marwood granted the request. There was a last-minute attack of nerves from the condemned man. Marwood put him at ease and assured him that he would feel no pain. He placed Charles Peace on the trapdoor and pulled the lever. According to Marwood the murderer 'passed like a summer's eve.'

Charles Peace spent very little time in Nottingham and yet the small Midlands town, in initiating a meeting between a master criminal and a female opportunist, ensured his eventual downfall and, perhaps inadvertently, facilitated his redemption.

10

Pierrepoint and the Low Part of Town: a Concise History of Nottingham's Most Notorious Slum and How it Helped Establish a Baleful Family Enterprise

In 1850 the governor of the Nottingham County Gaol said this of the part of Nottingham known as Narrow Marsh:

> The low part of the town, called the Marsh, which is close by the prison, is inhabited by the worst part of the population and their conversation, which is often of a very bad kind, being both obscene and profane, can be heard in the evening and through the night by all prisoners.

Until the closing decades of the eighteenth century, Narrow Marsh was a relatively picturesque place. Situated at the base of a cliff beneath an affluent part of Nottingham, houses in the Marsh were reasonably large and furnished with a garden apiece. The advent of industrialisation brought an unprecedented influx of workers from the fields and farms looking for higher wages and a better standard of living. Cheap new housing was needed. Old Narrow Marsh was replaced with tightly packed, congested back-to-backs and numerous lodging houses. The Marsh quickly became a concentration of courtyards connected by narrow alleyways with Red Lion Street at the cliff's base and Leenside, running parallel with the river, forming the area's borders. If the new occupants of the Marsh had any notions of exchanging the harshness of rural living for an urban utopia, they were soon to feel deeply cheated. Narrow Marsh was overcrowded and filthy. It fostered violence, vice and disease. It could almost have been deliberately conceived by a criminal imagination to incubate lawless behaviour.

Putting architectural design to one side, the topography of Narrow Marsh was dangerous without any assistance from man: the river Trent was prone to flooding at the best of times. Narrow Marsh was on the flood plain as it stood but was particularly vulnerable due to its close proximity to the river Leen. In 1770 the first few feet of the Marsh disappeared under water. In 1795, Narrow Marsh flooded again. For two days the Marsh was isolated from the rest of Nottingham and only reachable by boat.

In 1829 a section of the cliff face that overlooked Narrow Marsh collapsed and destroyed a sizable part of the street below. Signs of instability in the overhanging rocks had been evident for a few days prior to the fall. With the exception of a Mr Wright, who was adamant that there was nothing to fear, all of the vulnerable residents had evacuated their homes. At twenty minutes to eight in the evening, a piece of cliff weighing over 100 tonnes collapsed on top of Red Lion Street: five houses were destroyed.

A rooftop view of Narrow Marsh. (Picture courtesy of Nottingham City Council and www.picturethepast.org.uk)

A rooftop view of the Narrow Marsh site as it looks today.

Left: Red Lion Street, Narrow Marsh. (Picture courtesy of Nottingham City Council and www.picturethepast.org.uk)

Below: Modern Red Lion Street (now Cliff Road).

Joanna Ledwhich's audacious escape from Nottingham County Gaol almost cost her her life when the rope snapped and she fell into Narrow Marsh.

The traditionally despised forces of law and order worked with the locals to clear the rubble and rescue those who had been trapped: a young boy was pulled out of the ruins. Mercifully, nobody was killed.

The cliff face posed other problems: cut into the rock were caves that predated industrial Narrow Marsh. The caves were used for commercial purposes, with goods often being sold out of the cave mouths. Some of the caves were situated directly beneath the foundations of the County Gaol and were believed by the governor to be a direct threat to the prison's security.

Escape was a constant problem throughout the lifespan of the prison and escaped prisoners, once they had cleared the walls, would invariably head for the Marsh. Its labyrinthine design aided escapees and the slum's natural antipathy to the forces of law and order didn't hurt a fugitive's chances of escape either. In 1831 Joanna Ledwhich was sentenced to be transported for robbery. On 14 March she made a rope from bed sheets and a clothesline. She scaled the prison's inner wall unheeded and lowered herself over the other side. Part of the way down the seventy-foot drop, the rope snapped and Ledwhich fell into the Marsh. She survived the fall, suffering cuts and bruises, but sustaining no serious injury. Ledwhich got to her feet and made her escape aided by a friend waiting for her below. A number of people were said to have observed the escape. The inference seemed to be that nobody raised the alarm, aided the police or hindered the prisoner in anyway. Joanna Ledwhich was never recaptured.

The presence of the caves also inverted the traditional problem of escape, leaving the gaol actually susceptible to being broken into. During the Reform Bill Riots of 1831, the governor expressed fear that he could hear men beneath his gaol plotting an assault on the building. The attack never came, but his worries were not unfounded. Prisons were often

Bricked-up cave mouths on the borders of Narrow Marsh. These caves (situated beneath the County Gaol) were perceived as a threat to the prison's security as it was deemed possible to fill them with gunpowder and prime the gaol-house walls.

favourite targets of the mob during the riots of the period. In 1780 the London mob had famously stormed Newgate Prison during the Gordon Riots and released its prisoners. The Inspector of Prisons also noted in his annual report that the Narrow Marsh excavations were a possible vantage point from which to 'blow the place up.'

The more routine relationship between the gaol and the Marsh was that of deafening noise as well as the traffic of contraband items and information. The following excerpt comes from the journal of Nottingham County Gaol's governor:

Sunday Evening, June 17th, 1849 – Great disturbances in the Narrow Marsh during the night: the constables sprang their rattles[11] at midnight; the shouting, screaming, singing, &c., continued until morning.

Persons on the outside often call to the prisoners and make signals to them and prisoners in turn often call and make signals to people on the outside – Tobacco and notes are often flung over the walls to the prisoners and notes are in the same way sent by prisoners to their acquaintances on the outside. When there is noise, it is often very difficult to know whether it proceeds from the prison or from the persons on the outside.

---

11. Before whistles were introduced, police officers carried rattles (similar to those used in football matches today) to raise the alarm or call for assistance.

The Loggerheads pub, a notorious eighteenth and nineteenth-century meeting place for thieves and vagabonds.

The din was undeniably augmented by the presence of twelve public houses in Narrow Marsh. It is fair to surmise that most of these were rough places, but the worst was indisputably The Loggerheads. Situated on Red Lion Street, beneath the County Gaol, the pub's notorious reputation was summed up, once again, by the prison governor:

> There is a public house very near the prison, which is a notorious resort of thieves, and where there is often a great uproar, particular on Saturday and Sunday nights. Last Saturday night the noise in the Marsh was beyond everything, and it continued till after three in the morning. About the middle of the night there were cries of murder and some women were screaming. Such cries are frequent.

The problem of noise pollution paled into insignificance compared to the problems of actual pollution. The biggest threat to life and health in Narrow Marsh was undoubtedly the appalling sanitation. Families packed into tiny back-to-back housing shared a courtyard. The courtyard housed their toilet. The toilet in question was an ash privy, essentially a glorified hole in the ground, regularly occupied but infrequently emptied. Often there were only three or four toilets for every 250 people. The stench must have been unbelievable.

The occupants of a courtyard shared a supply of drinking water from an outside standpipe. The standpipe was often positioned close to a toilet. Narrow Marsh toilets were prone to leaking and often urine and faecal matter would trickle down, lapping around the base of the pipe. Narrow Marsh's water supply quickly became contaminated. In 1873 a survey revealed that of every

A memorial garden built over graves in memory of numerous cholera victims killed in the 1832 outbreak. The epidemic began in Narrow Marsh and spread throughout Nottingham claiming over 300 lives.

gallon of Narrow Marsh drinking water, 31.5 per cent was solid effluence. The consequences were frequently lethal. On 6 July 1832, a man in the Lees Yard area of Narrow Marsh contracted cholera. By October 1832 the disease had spread through the entire town infecting 900 people and killing 330. The victims' bodies were buried in three cemeteries especially constructed for fatalities of the epidemic. The largest of these was near Narrow Marsh.

By the 1850s, the entire population of Nottingham had swelled by 30 per cent. Areas like Narrow Marsh had their rapidly expanding populations squeezed and siphoned into whatever buildings were available. Although many paid rent for (or even owned) a single dilapidated property for their family, many others were obliged to stay in the Marsh's numerous common lodging houses. These establishments were boarding houses of the cheapest standard and lowest quality. An evening in one of these places might find a patron sharing a bed with a complete stranger, or else sleeping on the kitchen floor. If a bed wasn't available a patron might spend the night reclining on a dismantled door. Lodging houses saw a constant flow of human traffic, day and night. Because of the cheap overnight rates a lodging house was the ideal environment for a prostitute to practice her profession. Children frequently used them and sexual abuse was not unknown. Common lodging houses were initially designed for short term or overnight use, but in time they became the permanent homes of many Narrow Marsh residents. The official terminology for a lodging house denizen was 'inmate', a semantic indication of their standing in the social hierarchy of Nottingham, as little better than criminals or lunatics.

These were just the official lodging houses; there were many more unregistered establishments that specifically provided accommodation for professional criminals. The nineteenth century saw migratory communities of thieves, charlatans and conmen following various travelling fairs up

A yard in the neighbouring area of Middle Marsh but typical of the squalor found in Narrow Marsh. (Picture courtesy of Nottingham City Council and www.picturethepast.org.uk)

and down the country, preying on the crowds that they attracted. Thieves needed a place to stay when the fair was in town and Narrow Marsh was a favourite way station for the itinerant criminal. Bush's Lodging House in Narrow Marsh was notorious for the number of villains' names on its registration book. Bush's was unusual in that it was a legitimate, registered lodging house flagrantly catering for the criminal classes.

Criminal life ran concurrent with normal working life in the Marsh. Induction into a life of prostitution was a constant temptation for impoverished women. The Loggerheads public house was reputedly the ideal place to fence stolen goods. Children were especially vulnerable to criminal recruitment. Gangs of young thieves worked the Marsh and were surprisingly sophisticated. A favourite trick of theirs to evade capture by a pursuing police officer was to arrange to have clotheslines lowered at strategic moments during a chase. Clotheslines that normally hung above head-height were now positioned at the neck or chest-height of a charging policeman. The pursuing officer distracted by the chase would soon become entangled, or garrotted by a spider's web of clothes and rope. Adult criminals had little need of such elaborate strategies. It was less time-consuming to simply punch a police officer in the face if the police officer got in their way, enforcers of the law being generally held in contempt in Narrow Marsh. Many residents thought little of assaulting the police. Victorian police normally walked their beats alone, but Narrow Marsh police officers patrolled in pairs. Victorian police seldom carried firearms, but Narrow Marsh gas men did. Employees of the gas company, with the onerous duty of lighting the gas lamps in the Marsh, were issued with pistols for their own protection.

Narrow Marsh was a place where violence was endemic. It had a reputation for toughness unequalled in any other part of Nottingham. Fights, either between locals or outsiders, were

Narrow Marsh clotheslines were often lowered at strategic junctures by child thieves to entangle pursuing police officers. (Picture courtesy of Nottingham City Council and www.picturethepast.org.uk)

The area on the borders of Narrow Marsh where John Hutchinson murdered four-year-old Albert Matthews.

brutal with visiting gangs of brawlers routinely sent home licking their cuts and bruises. In 1907, a domestic argument between a husband and his wife resulted in the husband being stabbed in the neck and belly while the wife suffered cuts to the face and arms.

Death was a constant unwanted companion in the Marsh but murders were extremely rare. The odd body would surface from time to time, like that of George Boston, who was discovered in a closet in 1915. These corpses may well have been the consequence of premeditated murder, but as stonewalling the police was almost an article of faith for the residents of the Marsh, it was impossible to establish. Surprisingly there are only two documented murders in the entire history of the Marsh. Both murders were particularly horrific and happened within a few years of each other. The two murderers were easily arrested and hanged and present at both executions was Henry Pierrepoint, one of the first great hangmen of the twentieth century.

In 1905 an unemployed labourer and ex-soldier named John Hutchinson had been lodging with the Matthews family in Narrow Marsh. Hutchinson had been living there for less than a month. On 31 January, Hutchinson had spent much of the day in a public house drinking. He returned home in the early afternoon and was asked to look after the Matthews' four-year-old son Albert while the mother went to work. Albert's mother left Hutchinson alone with child at five o'clock. Two hours later Hutchinson was seen wandering the streets of the Marsh without the boy. He approached a police officer and confessed to having killed the child. Hutchinson led the police officer back to his lodgings and showed him the body. The boy had been beheaded and cut into pieces. Albert admitted his guilt, claiming that he had acted under provocation when the boy had thrown a poker at him.

When the case came to trial, Hutchinson's defence pleaded insanity. John Hutchinson's family had a history of mental illness; two relatives had previously been locked away in mental institutions. Four more family members had committed suicide. In addition to this, it transpired that Hutchinson himself suffered from fits and in his youth had sustained a serious head injury. The case for the defence had credibility, but Hutchinson's extensive medical history was of no interest to the jury, who took twenty minutes to find him guilty. The judge concurred and sentenced him to death. It would be Nottingham's first execution of the new century.

Hutchinson's hangman was John Billington. Billington's assistant was Henry Pierrepoint. The meeting of the two hangmen marked the unofficial passing of the baton from one executioner's dynasty to another.

John Billington was the son of James Billington, one of the last great executioners of the Victorian age. When William Marwood died in 1883, James applied to succeed him as England's principle hangman. He was only partially successful, managing instead to secure the position of hangman for Yorkshire. Although he held something approximating the post he craved, Billington had not yet accrued any experience, as nobody seemed to be committing murder in Yorkshire at that time. James' eagerness to acquire practical know-how caused him to throw his net further afield, bringing him briefly into Nottingham's orbit. Billington got wind of a killing that had recently taken place in the East Midlands town. He wrote to the Sheriff of Nottingham and effectively pitched for the post of hangman. Nottinghamshire did not have a resident executioner and it was their custom, whenever the need arose, to bring one in for the job. Billington boasted that he could erect a scaffold in one hour and could carry out a hanging without the aid of an assistant thus minimising expense. It was a fine sales pitch designed to undercut the opposition and it probably would have secured him the job had he not got his facts wrong – the crime in question was manslaughter and not murder. His services were not required on this occasion. In time, Billington eventually achieved his ambition and would go on to gain fame for hanging Charles Thomas Wooldrige, the inspiration for the nameless trooper sentenced to death in Oscar Wilde's *The Ballad of Reading Gaol*. James' sons John, William and Thomas all followed him into the profession.

Above: Jane Gamble's murder at the hands of former lover Edward Glynn took place near the junction of Popham Street and Leenside (now Canal Street).

Opposite: A portrait of hangman Henry Pierrepoint.

Henry Pierrepoint was a native of Yorkshire who had nurtured an ambition to be a hangman from youth. Initially he was employed as a mill worker and a butcher's apprentice. Pierrepoint used the butcher's training to his advantage. He wrote to the Home Secretary emphasising knowledge of anatomy as a qualifying factor in his prospective consideration for the post of hangman. His application was successful and resulted in an interview at Manchester Prison. Pierrepoint impressed the interview panel and was sent for two weeks' training at Newgate Prison in London. Training would have consisted of learning how to calculate a drop based on the height and weight of the condemned, how to set up and operate a gallows and how to apply the noose at the correct angle so as to break the neck. Once the basics were in place, Pierrepoint would have been subject to endless drills and simulations until a hanging could be performed with as much speed and accuracy as possible. In the beginning, Pierrepoint became assistant hangman to Thomas Billington. But it was with Thomas' brother John that Henry made his first official visit to Nottingham, for the hanging of John Hutchinson. A year later John Billington was dead and Henry would return again to Nottingham as a hangman in his own right.

Death plagued the Billington family in the early years of the twentieth century. In 1901 James and his wife died within a few months of each other. Thomas Billington died a year later. William Billington lived until 1934 but retired in 1905. John Billington's death in 1905 was almost certainly the consequence of a long-standing feud with another hangman, William Warbrick. Warbrick suffered an accident as assistant to James Billington when he fell through a gallows trapdoor. He had always blamed James for the accident and had held the entire family in contempt ever since. When William Warbrick and John Billington were obliged to work together, the accident happened again. This time John fell through the trapdoor. He died two months later, many believed this was a consequence of injuries sustained in a deliberately engineered fall.

The second Narrow Marsh murder occurred in 1905. A young woman named Jane Gamble was stabbed to death in a gas-lit street. The murderer's name was Edward Glynn. Glynn was a sailor. He was twenty-six years old and romantically involved with Gamble, but it was an abusive relationship and Gamble left him. Glynn pleaded with her to return, but she refused. On 3 March, Jane Gamble was walking along Leenside on the edge of Narrow Marsh. Glynn approached her from behind and knifed her in the back and neck. Two men witnessed the attack, pursued and overpowered Glynn, restraining him until he was arrested. Jane Gamble died a day later from her wounds. The attack was so ferocious that a piece of the murder weapon was later found embedded in her backbone.

Edward Glynn was tried, convicted of murder and sentenced to death. Glynn was executed by Henry Pierrepoint on 7 August 1906. According to the notes in Pierrepoint's diary, Glynn was 5ft 4¼in. tall and weighed 161lbs. From these figures Pierrepoint, calculated that the length of rope required to break Glynn's neck and kill him quickly would be 6ft 7in.

Henry's brother Thomas joined the Home Office lists in 1905 and carried out executions until 1946. Henry's son Albert followed suit and became the best-known hangman of the twentieth century. He served his post from 1932 until 1954. He executed many famous criminals of the period, and in the 1940s hanged numerous Nazi war criminals in the aftermath of the Nuremberg Trials.

Henry Pierrepoint returned to Nottingham once more in 1909 to execute Samuel Atherby for the murder of his common-law wife and three children.

According to the notes in Pierrepoint's diary, Atherby was 5ft 6in. tall and weighed 174lbs. From these figures, Pierrepoint calculated that the length of rope required to break Atherby's neck, thus killing him quickly, would be 6ft 6in. Henry Pierrepoint retired a year later. Thus, Nottingham (and Narrow Marsh in particular) had played its part in establishing the last great English hangman dynasty.

Narrow Marsh remained untouched by progress for the first quarter of the twentieth century. Throughout the Edwardian period, it resisted change, retaining all the characteristics that had marked it as one of the most feared and impoverished areas of Georgian and Victorian Nottingham. In 1932, the Slum Clearance Act was passed and Narrow Marsh was demolished. With the exception of the County Gaol, The Loggerheads public house and a few buildings on what was once Red Lion Street, virtually nothing of the old tenement remains today.

Bibliography

An Account of St Mary's Nottingham by J.C.F. Food
Antique Guns and Gun Collecting by Frederick Wilkinson
Bare Fist Fighters of the 18th and 19th Century 1704 -1861 by Dick Johnson
Bible Commentary Old Testament by Warren Wiersbe
Bold as a Lion the Life of Bendigo – Champion of England by J.P. Bean
Broadsheet for the Execution of William Saville, 1844
The Case Book of Sherlock Holmes by Arthur Conan Doyle
The Case of John Darrell Minister and Exorcist by Corinne Holt Rickert
A Centenary History of Nottingham: an A-Z of Local History edited by John Beckett
Chilling True Tales of Old London by Keith Johnson
Con Men and Cutpurses: Scenes from the Hogarthian Underworld edited by Lucy Moore
Conveyance of Nottingham Prison in the County of
Discovering Highwaymen by Russell Ash
Edward II 1307-1327 by Mary Saeler
The Elizabethan Underworld by Gamin Salgado
The English Highwayman a Legend Varnished by Peter Haining
Executioner Pierrepoint: An Autobiography by Albert Pierrepoint
The Fifty Most Amazing Crimes of the Last One Hundred Years edited by J.M. Parrish and John R. Crossland
The Great Prize Fight by Alan Lloyd
A History of Britain at the Edge of the World 300 BC-AD 1603 by Simon Sharma
The History Today Companion to British History edited by Juliet Gardiner and Neil Wenborn
The Hangman's Record Volume One by Steve Fielding
The Hangman's Record Volume Two by Steve Fielding
Hangmen of England: a History of Execution from Jack Ketch to Albert Pierrepoint by Brian Bailey
Henry Pierrepoint's Diary
Highwaymen and Outlaws by Michael Billett
Isabella and the Strange Death of Edward II by Paul Doherty
Isabella She Wolf of France, Queen of England by Alison Weir
The Illustrated Book of Guns and Rifles edited by Frederick Wilkinson
The Illustrated Book of Pistols by Frederick Wilkinson
Inspectors of Prisons Reports for England
John Darrell – Exorcist by R.A. Mardant
John Howard's Prison Reports
The Lancashire Witch Craze – Janet Preston and the Lancashire Witches 1612 by Jonathan Lumby

The Last Plantagenets by T.B. Costain
The Lesson of the Scaffold: The Public Execution Controversy In Victorian England by David D. Cooper
London the Executioner's City by David Brandon and Alan Brooke
Moby Dick by Herman Melville
Newark Advertiser
The Newgate Calendar
Nottingham: A Place of Execution from 1201 – 1908 by Terry Lambley
Nottinghamshire Constabulary 150 Years in Photographs by Bill Withers
The Nottingham Date Book
Nottingham Evening Post Bygones Specials: The Sinister Side of Nottingham, Narrow Marsh, Crime and Punishment
Nottingham's Royal Castle and Ducal Palace by Andrew Hamilton
Nottingham…The Sinister Side by Steve Jones
Oscar Wilde by Richard Ellmann
The Oxford History of the Prison edited by Norval Morris and David J. Rothman
Reports of Gaols, 1833
Riot, Risings and Revolution: Governance and Violence in Eighteenth- Century England by Ian Gilmour
The Scotsman (26 February 2005)
Stand and Deliver: a History of Highway Robbery by David Brandon
The Shire Hall and Old County Gaol by Ken Brand
Victorian Murders by Roy Harley Lewis
Victorian Prison Lives by Phillip Priestly
Victorian Sensation or the Spectacular, the Shocking and the Scandalous in Nineteenth Century Britain by Michael Diamond
The Victorian Underworld by Kellow Chesney
Victorian Underworld by Ronald Thomas
Websites: The Straight Dope, Wikepedia, nottshistory.org.uk, museumstore.the Alamo.org/star, Civil War Time and Antiques Review

'Possibly the worst time in English legal history to be an incompetent thief...'

A Gallery of Punishments and Prison Life

Prison warder, *c.* 1900. (All photographs featured in this section are courtesy of the Galleries of Justice; they form part of the unique collection of images presented in *The Prison Service in Britain* by Beverley Baker and Laura Butler.)

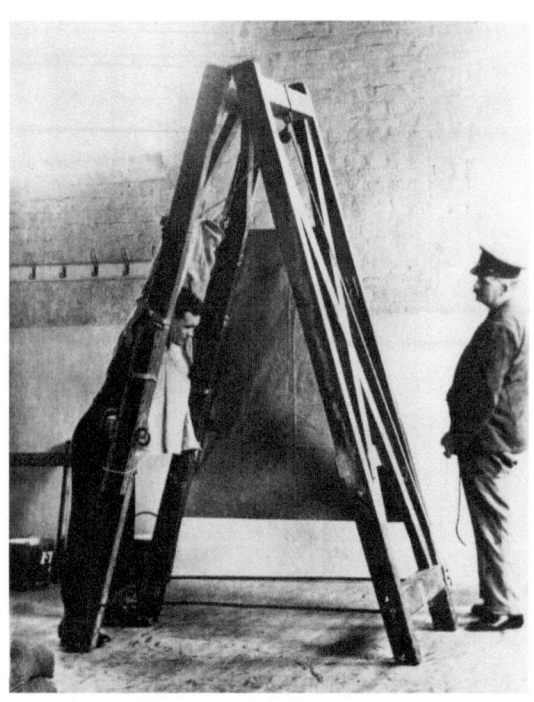

This page: Images of the whipping frame and the different ways it was put to use. Floggings were administered with a 'cat-o'-nine-tails' or a birch.

Opposite, above left: A Wormwood Scrubs inmate turning the crank – a machine with a handle that had to be turned a certain amount of times a day and a form of useless labour.

Opposite, above right: Another form of labour was picking oakum (old tar-soaked rope) – intended to break both the body and spirit of the prisoner.

Opposite, below: The treadmill was invented by Mr Cubitt and was first used in 1817 as a form of useless labour.

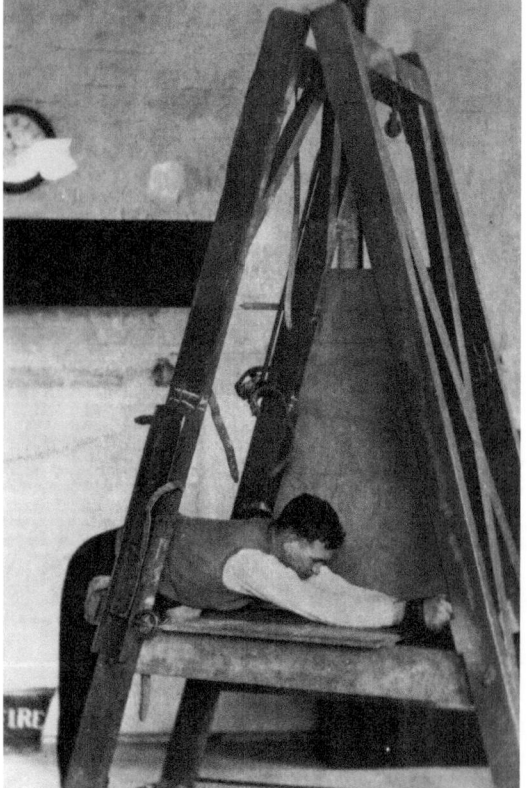

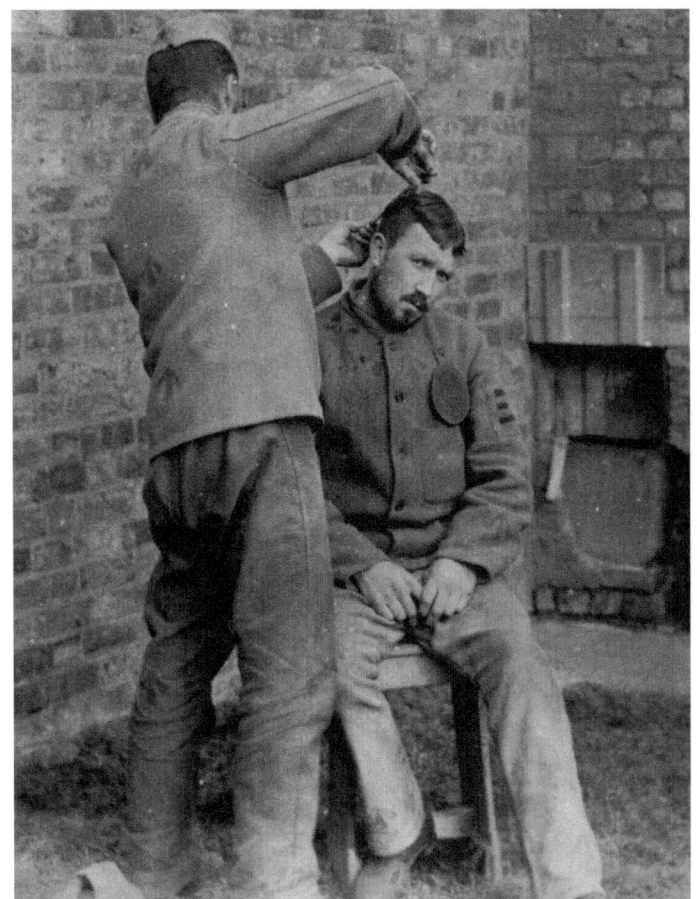

Opposite: Mugshot album, 1898-1903.

Right: Hair used to be cropped short on arrival, as shown here in around 1900. This was to prevent the spread of lice, but also served to take away the prisoner's individuality.

Below: The range of prohibited items found in prisons can be quite astonishing...

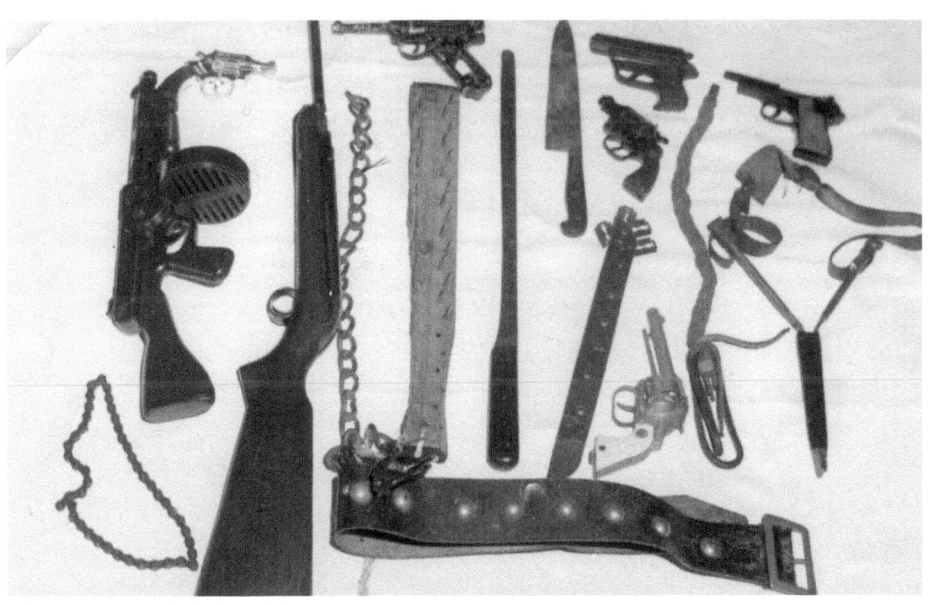

Other local titles published by Tempus

The Prison Service in Britain
BEVERLEY BAKER AND LAURA BUTLER

From the days when prisoners worked out their sentences at the crank, in the silence of solitary confinement, the changes have been vast – as recorded in this fascinating photographic collection. Featuring archive images of prisoners and 'screws', incarcerated mothers and formidable governors and the cells and schoolrooms where inmates passed the hours, the book records every aspect of prison life, providing a unique insight into the history of the penal service.

978 07524 4190 0

Murder & Crime in Lancashire
MARTIN BAGGOLEY

Lavishly illustrated with contemporary illustrations, this fascinating selection of tales of murder and manslaughter from across Lancashire spans more than 200 years of criminal history. The crimes are as diverse as the locations in which they were committed, and include mass murder and suicide in Salford, infanticide in Manchester, a wager that turned to vicious assault in Liverpool and a sweetheart shot to death in Southport – making this a shocking and compelling account of the Red Rose county's darker side.

978 07524 4358 4

The 'Haunts' of Robin Hood
JILL ARMITAGE

Old England was a country of vast, impenetrable woodland. In the dark, uncharted realm of Sherwood Forest grew the legend of Robin Hood – but is this where he still remains? Passing through hidden caves and ancient abbeys, this book searches all the settings of the old ballads for something more than tangible: the ghosts who haunt these romantic locations. Lavishly illustrated with more than 100 photographs, the book provides a pictorial tour of the rich folklore of Robin Hood Country.

978 07524 4331 7

Murder & Crime in Pendle and the Ribble Valley
JACQUELINE DAVITT

Illustrated with more than sixty photographs and drawing upon a variety of sources including police, court and even church records, this collection of true tales from across the Ribble Valley provides a fascinating record of crime and punishment in the area over the last 300 years. From the Pendle witches' dark magic to petty theft and the drunken crimes of 'talking too loudly' and 'jumping on the pavement', the book catalogues a chilling range of misdeeds which will horrify and captivate anyone interested in the criminal history of the area.

978 07524 4495 6

If you are interested in purchasing other books published by Tempus, or in case you have difficulty finding any Tempus books in your local bookshop, you can also place orders directly through our website

www.tempus-publishing.com